Augustine F. Hewit

The King's Highway

Third Edition

Augustine F. Hewit

The King's Highway
Third Edition

ISBN/EAN: 9783744773775

Printed in Europe, USA, Canada, Australia, Japan

Cover: Foto ©Lupo / pixelio.de

More available books at **www.hansebooks.com**

THE KING'S HIGHWAY

OR

The Catholic Church the Way of Salvation

AS

REVEALED IN THE HOLY SCRIPTURES

"And a path and a Way shall be there; and it shall be called the Holy Way: and this shall be unto you a straight way, so that fools shall not err therein."—ISAIAS XXXV. 8.

BY THE

VERY REV. AUGUSTINE F. HEWIT, D.D.

Of the Congregation of St. Paul

THIRD EDITION

NEW YORK
THE CATHOLIC BOOK EXCHANGE
120 West 60th Street

1893

Printed at The Columbus Press, 120 West 60th St.

PREFACE.

I HAVE written this book from the prompting of a desire to do something expressly for the benefit of that class of Protestants among whom I was born and brought up. Most of the books written in English, with the direct object of convincing Protestants of the truth of the Catholic religion, are specially adapted to the use of Episcopalians of high-church opinions. And, moreover, those Catholic writers who make it their aim to convince and convert non-Catholics in general, without special reference to the small body of high-churchmen, usually have in view those who are on the extreme left of Protestantism, or have already lapsed into rationalism. The greater number of converts in our own day have been either from the one or the other of these two classes. Very few have passed directly from Calvinism, or the stricter form of what is called Evangelical Protestantism, to the Catholic faith. There have been, nevertheless, some conversions of persons of this sort in Scotland, England, and our own country, besides a much greater number in Germany. It is to be hoped that the light of divine truth and grace will ere long penetrate this body, which represents the dogmatic and historical Protestantism of the first pretended reformers, and has hitherto remained so apparently inert and immovable in the place where it was thrown by the convulsion of the sixteenth century. That it has begun to be disorganized and is on the way to complete disruption, is manifest. It must disappear in the common rationalism and infidelity of the age, or be reunited to the Catholic Church. All human and secondary causes are working toward the effect of producing the former most sad and disastrous result. It is only the grace and special providence of God which can prevent or impede it. It is to be hoped that this divine power will be shown, by bringing back at least a large number of those who still believe in the Bible and the divinity of Jesus Christ, with their offspring, to the fold of the true church, from which they are now separated by the sin of their ancestors.

I have determined to make one humble effort toward persuading those who are of the more noble sort, who really love truth and cling to their Christian traditions of faith and morals, to examine their position seriously, and carefully consider whether it is safe and durable for themselves and their children. I address only those who believe that those Scriptures of the Sacred Canon which are commonly received among orthodox Protestants and contained in their Bibles are really the word of God. I have in view, first of all, those who hold the Calvinistic doctrines, and, secondarily, all those who believe in common with Calvinists, without holding all their peculiar tenets, certain fundamental doctrines retained by Calvin, Luther, and the founders of the English Church. Those who hold more latitudinarian opinions are welcome to get what good they can from my course of arguing; but I have not made any attempt at directly convincing them on their own ground. My argument is from the Scriptures, and presupposes that their true sense, as held by the Catholic Church, is already in several things admitted, and in all other things must be admitted as absolute truth so soon as it is certainly known to be the true sense of the sacred writers. In my quotations I have used King James's Version, because it is the one with which my Protestant readers are familiar. At the same time, I have taken care to ascertain that the passages quoted are substantially correct renderings of the original texts, and have occasionally made some remarks to make the sense of the words used more obvious and precise. The number of non-Catholics who really believe that the Scriptures are the word of God, and must be taken as of divine authority, is rapidly diminishing. It is still, however, large and respectable, and includes a number of men whose learning and ability are eminent, and have been exerted in producing excellent works in defence of revealed religion against infidelity and rationalism. Therefore, although it is true that the controversy between the Catholic Church and old-fashioned Protestantism is rapidly losing its significance, it is not true that it has altogether lost it. The great controversy is with infidelity. Yet it is still worth our while to address argument and persuasion to those who hold on to a part of Christianity, and to reason with them on the evidence which proves that Catholicity is the true and perfect Christianity, the religion of the Bible, and the religion of the old forefathers of our faith. These persons look with dread and sorrow at the inroads of infidelity and immorality. They cling with a strong conviction and an ardent attachment to the belief in God, in revelation, in Jesus Christ as a divine Saviour, in the divine mission of the prophets and apostles, in the immortality of the soul, the resurrection, and the life to come. They ought to be completely and openly on our side. Unhappily, they are with our enemies, who are also theirs. Consciously, or unconsciously, they are in the position of the moderates of the French Revolution, accomplices in a rebellion, whose extreme advocates they are helping on in a warfare against God and his church, destined to become themselves the victims of their fury, if their warfare is successful. It is to be hoped that they will see this before the time of the approaching final conflict, and take their place in the Catholic ranks. Future events, however, can only be known in the future time. One thing we may, however, hope for with confidence: that many individuals will be converted to the church from those sects which follow the doctrines of Luther and Calvin. If so many have been converted from Anglicanism and rationalism, why should not a similar stream of conversion soon set in from this other direction? The movement toward the church has reached those others first, for obvious reasons. But at the present time the Catholic Church is so conspicuously brought before the minds of all men, everywhere; and is so rapidly extending itself in the regions where the old Presbyterianism and Congregationalism have held dominion; that the sincere, candid, and earnestly religious cannot help giving it their serious consideration. I have endeavored to stimulate and assist this conscientious enquiry in the following pages. I was brought up in

Calvinism, and studied the Calvinistic theology. I made a sincere effort to believe it, and to find in it a doctrine satisfactory to my reason, conscience, and heart. The result of my studies and prayers and efforts to find out and fulfil the will of God was that I became, through the divine grace, a Catholic. I shall be most happy if I can assist others to follow the same course and obtain a share in the same great blessing. Having myself passed over the road from Calvinism to the Catholic faith, I know it well ; and I am confident that all those who are disposed to follow the same route will receive great assistance from what I have written in the present volume. It is by means of those great Catholic doctrines which they already believe that I aim to show them the inconsistency of the errors which they hold with these aforementioned doctrines; and by means of their implicit Catholic principles and natural good sense that I endeavor to prove by deduction from those doctrines and express testimonies of Holy Scripture other Catholic doctrines which they misunderstand and reject. The mortal principle of the heresy of Luther is his doctrine of justification. Therefore I have made it my first object to refute that false and absurd tenet; and to prove the true and Catholic doctrine of justification, as the vital principle of the sound and orthodox doctrine of salvation through Jesus Christ. From this interior principle and doctrine I have proceeded outward to the exterior body and surface of the Catholic Church, instead of the usual method of beginning with the outward and visible, and going inward to that which is its invisible and spiritual form. This method is the most suitable for the class of persons I wish to reach, and for my chief object; which is, to present the Catholic Church, not so much in its historic truth and grandeur, as a divine institution for a certain general end and good; as in its relation to each individual soul, as the way and means of its eternal salvation. I offer this book, therefore, to those who wish to save their souls, and entreat of them to read it with a serious motive, and with prayer to God for light to see and good-will to obey the truth.

Its concluding pages and preface have been written amid the charming silence and solitude of the shores of that beautiful lake * whose original and Christian name was given to it on the day of its discovery, the eve of Corpus Christi, by the heroic martyr, Father Isaac Jogues. I have had the happiness of laying the corner-stone of the first Catholic church on the borders of the lake, the site of which is in the midst of scenes of historic interest, where formerly the sounds of bloody warfare were loud and frequent. On a still and bright Sunday afternoon, the magic panorama of nature wearing its softest and most attractive aspect, the air laden with the fragrance of sweet-fern, the psalms and litanies of the Roman Ritual were chanted, and the foundations of the Church of Caldwell, dedicated to the Sacred Heart of Jesus, were blessed. A crowd of Catholics and Protestants, including the offspring of various races and nations, white, colored, and Indian, picturesquely mingled together, devoutly partook in or listened with respectful and curious interest to the solemn prayers and psalmody, and gave attentive ears to the eloquent voice of the preacher, whose

* Lake George.

discourse closed the services of this auspicious day. In memory of this event, I dedicate this book to the Sacred Heart of Jesus in the Blessed Sacrament, with the prayer that it may become the corner-stone of many new sanctuaries consecrated to His glory in the hearts of my readers.

St. Mary's of the Lake,
    Lake St. Sacrament,
Fifteenth Sunday after Pentecost, Sept. 6, 1874.

CONTENTS.

CHAPTER FIRST.

PAGE

Fundamental Doctrines which are assumed as granted—The Calvinistic Doctrines of Particular Redemption, Election, and Reprobation refuted—The Way of Salvation through the Merits of Christ prepared for all Mankind—The Necessity of Special Means and Conditions by which the Redemption of the Human Race may be applied to Individual Men, . 17

CHAPTER SECOND.

Justification by Faith—The Lutheran and Calvinistic Doctrine of Justification by Faith alone refuted—The Nature and Office of Faith as the first Prerequisite to Justification explained—Statement and Proof of the Catholic Doctrine concerning Saving Faith, ... 66

CHAPTER THIRD.

Other Prerequisites of Justification—Repentance and Conversion to God—The Formal Cause and the Instruments of Justification—Regeneration and Sanctifying Grace—The Sacraments Instruments of Grace—Baptism the Sacrament of Regeneration, ... 81

CHAPTER FOURTH.

Necessity of Means for the Remission of Sin after Baptism—Venial and Mortal Sin—The Sacrament of Penance—Extreme Unction—Purgatory—Means for the Preservation and Increase of Grace and Holiness—The Holy Eucharist the great Source of Grace and Nourishment for the Soul, . 127

CHAPTER FIFTH.

Of the Church—Its Unity and Authority—Of the Rule of Faith—The Mystics—Luther's Doctrine of Private Illumination—Of Teaching Authority in General—Of Infallibility—Various Theories Examined and Tested—The Validity of the Argument from Scripture Established—Indirect, Negative, Cumulative, and Presumptive Proofs that the Catholic Church alone is the true Church, . . 163

CHAPTER SIXTH.

PAGE

The Nature, Attributes, and Organic Principles of the True Church proved from Scripture—Proof that the Holy, Catholic, Apostolic, Roman Church is the One True Church founded by Jesus Christ—The only Way of Salvation is in the Catholic Church—Conclusion, ... 337

THE WAY OF SALVATION.

CHAPTER FIRST.

Fundamental Doctrines which are assumed as granted—The Calvinistic Doctrines of Particular Redemption, Election, and Reprobation refuted—The Way of Salvation through the Merits of Christ prepared for all Mankind—The Necessity of Special Means and Conditions by which the Redemption of the Human Race may be applied to Individual Men

THE theme of my argument in the present volume is the way of salvation which is proposed in the Holy Scriptures, especially in those of the New Testament, and still more specifically in the Epistles of St. Paul the Apostle, who is the great Doctor of Grace. The particular scope of the argument does not, nevertheless, embrace the proof of all the doctrines involved in this theme, considered in all its completeness. Several of the most fundamental of these doctrines will be taken for granted at the outset, and assumed as the data from which the argument will proceed. The reason for doing so is, that the argument is addressed to those only who hold these doctrines as the first principles of their religious belief, and therefore do not require to have them proved. The chief of these doctrines which are taken as fully admitted by those who are addressed in this volume are: The Trinity, the Incarnation and Redemption, Original Sin, Salvation by Gratuitous Grace, and the Eternal Rewards and Punishments of the Future Life. The Way of Salvation is, consequently, determined to be a way provided by the pure and gratuitous goodness of God, through the Eternal Son made man and crucified for men; through which some men are saved from the guilt and penalty of sin, which binds all other members of the human race for ever, and are finally brought to the end of eternal beatitude in God. Most clearly, then, the only part of the general theme which remains as the topic of an argument, is the order or method according to which that salvation which proceeds from the merits of Jesus Christ and the grace of God, is applied to individual members of the human race. It is certain that whoever will be saved must be saved by the grace of Jesus Christ. But how is this grace to be obtained, and what are the conditions requisite on the part of man that it may be actually efficacious to his salvation? This is what is meant in these pages by the Way of Salvation. It is the way by which one who is con**vinced** that he needs to be saved, and who **desires** to be saved, may obtain with certainty the remission of sin, the grace and friendship of God, and everlasting life through the Divine Mediator Jesus Christ. That there is such a way, by which, in the words of St. Augustine, "all who are liberated are most certainly liberated," will be admitted without any question. But the question does arise, and must be answered at the outset, whether this way is open to all men without distinction, and to every individual of the human race without any exception. I shall therefore begin my exposition of the scheme of human salvation proposed in the Holy Scriptures precisely at this point.

The decree of Almighty God to provide a way of salvation for men, after the fall of Adam, included the whole human race without any exception, and consequently the redemption effected by Jesus Christ included all men without exception. I lay down this proposition as one to be proved by the Scripture. It has two parts: the first, that God decreed to provide and open a way of salvation for all men; and the second, that Jesus Christ actually accomplished what God decreed should be done, by his obedience unto death and his crucifixion. These two parts, however, although distinct, are inseparably connected together, and whatever proof is given of either one separately proves equally the other, and thus proves the entire complex proposition. For, whatever God decreed Jesus Christ accomplished, and no more; and whatever Jesus Christ accomplished, no less and no more was decreed by God. If God willed to provide salvation for all men, then Christ died for all; and if he died for all, then God willed that he should die to provide for all a way of salvation.

The evidence from the divine Scripture for both parts of the proposition is very abundant and clear. The particular texts which declare the great and consoling truth that Jesus Christ died for all men according to the eternal decree of the Father, will be more intelligible, if we first consider one primary and essential principle of all God's dealings with men. This principle is, that in the state of original justice, in the fall, and in the restoration, mankind bears a common relation to God and to the end which God has prefixed to the human race, and is treated as one grand whole, and not as a mere collection of separate individuals. The covenant of life which God made with Adam included all his posterity. The fall of Adam involved all his descendants in its consequences. The new covenant of remission and restoration to life was made by the Father with the Son, as the predestined head of the human race in his humanity. Jesus Christ is the second Adam, who undoes the ruinous work of the first Adam. The sin of Adam is the primary cause of the temporal and eternal miseries of the human race from which Jesus Christ came to redeem it. It was, therefore, this sin before all others which he expiated on the cross. And, in expiating this original sin, he expiated all other sins, for the satisfaction which he made to the divine justice covered the whole ground of the debt due to God by men for their sins. All mankind fell in Adam and was redeemed by Jesus Christ, is a condensed summary of that part of the theology of the Scriptures which concerns the relation of the human race, under the present order of providence, to God. And this I will now proceed to prove explicitly, so far as relates to my present topic.

The first passage I cite is that portion of the First Epistle of St. Paul to Timothy, which is included within the first six verses of the second chapter.

"I exhort therefore, that, first of all, supplications, prayers, intercessions, and giving of thanks, be made for all men; for kings, and for all that are in authority; that we may lead a quiet and peaceable life in all godliness and honesty. For this is acceptable in the sight of God our Saviour; *who will have all men to be saved*, and to come unto the knowledge of the truth. For there is one God, and one mediator between God and men, the man

Christ Jesus; *who gave himself a ransom for all,* to be testified in due time."

The meaning of this passage is obvious on its very surface, but becomes much more clear on a closer inspection. The commandment is given to pray for all men, and the reason on which that commandment is founded is the will of God that all men should attain salvation. The will of God to save men is therefore coextensive with the precept to pray for men. Is the latter universal and without exception, the former must be equally universal, and extend to every individual of the human race. There is no possible way of restricting the will of God to save men, and the extent of the ransom offered for men, except by restricting the precept of praying for men to a certain class. This can only be done by a violent interpretation, which I trust the good sense of every one of my readers will reject. One who wishes to restrict the saving will of God and the ransom of Christ to the elect, may say—namely, that the end of the prayer for all men is merely that "we," meaning the elect, "may lead a quiet and peaceable life." Even if this were granted, there still remains the statement that "God will have *all men* to be saved," which cannot be restricted in its meaning without some reason derived from the context, or the nature of the case treated of, which requires such a restriction. Then, again, the following clause, "and to come unto the knowledge of the truth," shows that the reason for praying was not exclusively that the faithful of that present time, the church, who are most naturally understood by the word "we," might enjoy peace; but that others, who were then numbered among the heathen, might also be converted. The special motive, therefore, which is given for praying for rulers—namely, that they might, through the effect of the prayers of the faithful, leave them in peace—does not qualify the entire passage in which they are commanded to pray for all men. The reason why they should pray for all men in general is that God will have all men to be saved, and the special reason why they should pray for rulers is that they may leave Christians in undisturbed liberty to profess and practise their religion. And this is confirmed by the universal understanding and consequent practice of this precept by Christians in all times and places. They have always been in the habit of offering both public and private prayers for all men without distinction or exception, sinners and unbelievers included, that all may come to the knowledge and love of the truth and be saved. The obvious sense of the passage may therefore be thus expressed. The apostle commands that prayers should be offered for all men; and in particular for rulers, that they may so govern as to leave Christians the free and peaceful exercise of their rights of conscience. The reason and motive why Christians should pray for all men is that they should have charity towards the whole human race, in imitation of the love of God and of Jesus Christ towards men, which is universal. This is still further established and confirmed by the reasons which are given in conclusion for this universal love on the part of God and of Jesus Christ towards men. The first reason given is, that "there is one God," or, in other words, that all men have the same Creator and Sovereign Lord, who is the author of salvation, or, as St. Paul expresses it, is "God our Saviour." The second reason is, that there is "one mediator between God and men, the man Christ Jesus; who gave himself a ransom for all." As Jesus Christ is possessed of the worth of condignity with God the Father by his divine nature, and is therefore the sole and sufficient mediator in respect to God, so, by his human nature, he is made a suitable mediator in respect to men. And because he has taken that human nature which is common to all men, he is the mediator of all men, and, as the apostle declares, without restriction, "gave himself a ransom for all." It is only necessary, therefore, to have human nature in order to come under that merciful providence of "God our Saviour" which is called the order of salvation, and to be *ipso facto* included in the mediation of Christ and in the number of that multitude for whose sins, both original and actual, he gave himself as a ransom. The whole passage brings out most clearly the idea which is found everywhere in the Scriptures, that God is in a special and proper sense the God of the human race. God is the God of men, because he has preferred men before all other creatures. He is not merely good and just toward them, but also merciful, providing a way of forgiveness for them when they sin, and of salvation when they have lost themselves, and is therefore for them, and for them alone, God the Saviour. The reason of it is found in their human nature, the predestined nature of the Eternal Son, which is made the nature of God by the hypostatic union in his Person. God the Father loves all men, in a special sense, because they partake of the nature of his Son. Jesus Christ loves them because they partake of his own nature, are his race, and of one blood with himself. This relation to Jesus Christ as the mediator and to the Father as God the Saviour is contracted by that generation from Adam which makes each individual man a member of the human race, and by virtue of this relationship every man is made a capable and fit subject of the mercy of God and the grace of Christ. The two lines by which the whole multitude of human individuals are connected with Adam and with Christ are therefore parallel and coextensive. That same multitude to which God decreed the salvation by original justice which was lost in the fall is the multitude for which he decreed to provide a way of salvation through the mediation and redemption of his Son. St. Paul frequently draws this parallel, and argues with great force from one member of it to the other.

In his Second Epistle to the Corinthians (v. 14), he argues that all men had incurred spiritual death, from the truth, well known to his auditors as a doctrine pertaining to the Christian faith, that Christ died for all men. "We thus judge that, if one died for all, then were all dead." This judgment of the apostle is the conclusion of an informal syllogism, which, reduced to a regular form, is the following: All those to whom pertains the redemption merited by the death of Jesus Christ died in the first Adam, and need restoration to life by the second Adam. But this redemption pertains to all men. Therefore, all men died in the first Adam, etc. The minor premiss in this syllogism—"this redemption pertains to all men," which is the same in substance with the express words of the apostle, "one died for all"—may be, therefore, expanded into the following proposition: The redemption merited by the death of Jesus Christ pertains to all those who, being dead in the first Adam, need restoration to life by the second Adam—that is, to all men without exception.* And, in the nineteenth following verse of the same chapter, we have a further confirmation of the universality of this truth in St. Paul's declaration: "God was in Christ, reconciling *the world* unto himself."

In the very thicket of the "things hard to be understood" which crowd the central peak of St. Paul's Epistles, the fifth chapter of the Epistle to the Romans, this same universal way to salvation is seen threading the summits of the mysteries of theology, so plain, so clear, so unmistakable, that even "the wayfaring man, though a fool, need not err therein." (15) "If through the offence of one many be dead" (ὁι πολλοι, the multitude of all men): "much more the grace of God, and the gift by grace, which is by one man, Jesus Christ, hath abounded unto many" (εἰς τους πολλους, to the same multitude). (18) "As by the offence of one judgment came upon *all men* to condemnation: even so by the righteousness of one the free gift came upon *all men* unto justification of life." The New York Bible Society's edition of King James's Bible (minion ref. 16mo, 2d ed., 1861) here refers to two parallel passages. The first is St.

* Vid. Franzelin, "De Deo," Thesis xxxvii.; "De Volunt. Salvif. Anteced."

John xii. 32, "And I, if I be lifted up, will **draw all men** unto me." The second is Heb. ii. 9, "But we see Jesus, who was made a little lower than the angels for the suffering of death, crowned with glory and honor; that he by the grace of God should *taste death for every man.*" In another place St. Paul declares: "We trust in the living God, who is the *Saviour of all men*, specially of those that believe."* Here the perverse interpretation of those who explain the universal terms used in the passages cited above as referring only to the whole multitude of the elect is expressly excluded. For, while the apostle distinctly teaches that the faithful participate in the benefits of the redemption in a much higher sense than other men, he nevertheless declares with equal distinctness that God is the Saviour of that entire multitude which includes all other men as well as those who believe. So also does the apostle St. John, in a number of other passages besides the remarkable one quoted a little above: "In him was life; and the life was the light of men"; "That was the true Light, which lighteth every man that cometh into the world"; "Behold the Lamb of God, which taketh away the sin of the world"; "And he is the propitiation for our sins: and not for ours only, but also for the sins of the whole world"; "And we have seen and

---

* 1 Tim. iv. 10.

do testify that the Father sent the Son to be the Saviour of the world."*

Besides these passages, which are in themselves perfectly clear and sufficient, there are many others distinctly affirming that Christ died for many who will never obtain everlasting life, and therefore with equal precision excluding the false and heretical doctrine that he died for the elect only. This may be seen by reading the Epistles, which are addressed to the whole body of those who profess the Christian faith, and have been received into the church by baptism. Everywhere, their especial happiness, as partakers of the benefits of Christ's death, and their consequent obligation and encouragement to fidelity, are enlarged upon with the greatest copiousness and force. At the same time they are warned of the danger to which they are exposed of forfeiting all these blessings, and incurring the judgments of God, if they draw back and do not persevere. By themselves these passages prove only that Christ died for a great number of men besides those who are predestined to everlasting life, at least for all who are baptized, who obtain the gift of faith, and are justified. That many are really included among the faithful and receive the gifts of grace who are not finally saved, and therefore that the number of the justified is

* John i. 4, 9, 29. 1 Ep. John ii. 2 ; iv. 14.

not identical with the number of the predestined, will be proved hereafter. And in that connection, the proof from Scripture will be given that God wills the salvation of those who are only temporarily justified, and that Jesus Christ died for them, as well as for those who persevere. This is a subaltern proposition to the more general proposition which I am at present engaged in proving. Its special proof is equally conclusive with that of the principal proposition against the contrary proposition of Calvinists and Jansenists. We shall see a little later that it destroys the entire Calvinistic theory of particular redemption and exclusive grace for the elect, and confirms the evidence otherwise given of the universal extension of the decree of redemption to the whole human race. Throughout the entire Scripture, the invitations and exhortations addressed to all those to whom the divine revelation is made known, and the declarations of the willingness of God to grant remission of sins to all who are penitent, are founded upon the universality of the mercy of God toward men. We have already seen that St. Paul argues from the fundamental truth of one God, the creator of all men, to the universality of his merciful providence over all. "There is one God, who will have all men to be saved." In like manner, the same apostle asks, with the confidence of one who appeals to something well known and indisputable, "Is he the God of the Jews only? is he not also of the Gentiles?" And again he declares that "the same Lord over all is rich unto all that call upon him. For whosoever shall call upon the name of the Lord shall be saved." * The name "Father of mercies" belongs, therefore, to God by virtue of a common relation of all men to him, and not by virtue of a special relation of some favored and select number of men. The Psalms are crowded with aspirations of praise to God for his goodness and mercy, and the key to the proper interpretation of all these inspired breathings of the royal Psalmist of Israel is given by one remarkable passage: "The Lord is *good to all*, and his tender mercies are over *all his works*." †

This proposition is absolutely universal, and affirms that goodness flows out of an essential attribute of God upon all rational creatures without exception. So far as concerns men, while their earthly probation lasts, this goodness takes the specific form of mercy toward sinners. "As I live, saith the Lord God, I have no pleasure in the death of the wicked; but that the wicked turn from his way and live." ‡ "The Lord is not slack concerning his promise, as some men count slackness; but

---

* Rom. iii. 29; x. 12, 13.   † Ps. cxliv. (Prot. cxlv.) 9.
‡ Ezech. xxxiii. 11.

is long-suffering to us-ward, not willing that any should perish, but that all should come to repentance."*

It must be plain to every attentive reader of the foregoing pages, especially if he be already familiar with the Holy Scriptures, that the most special acts of goodness and mercy on the part of God toward any of his rational creatures are merely applications of a universal good-will toward all, which is necessarily implied in the act of creation, and proceeds from the essential nature of God. The ultimate reason why God has so highly exalted St. Michael the Archangel, Abraham, David, the Blessed Virgin Mary, is, that he is good to his creatures; he loves that which he has made. Although it is not necessary that God should create any rational beings, yet it is necessary that, if he determines to create them, he should love them, and provide them with sufficient means to attain their end. In this respect all are equal before God, and must be impartially treated. The discrimination among creatures is one which respects the kind and amount of good to be conferred on each genus, species, or individual, and not their antecedent division into two classes, the elect and the reprobate, the first created for happiness, and the second for misery. The only genera and species of rational

* 2 Pet. iii. 9.

creatures whose existence is known to us are angels and men. The goodness of God toward the angels was shown by giving them a perfect nature adorned with grace, and the opportunity of attaining the vision of God by a short probation, but without any possibility of reversing their choice when it was once made. It was, therefore, the antecedent will of God that all the angels should be saved, and those who forfeited salvation were excluded from it purely on account of their own wilful and deliberate disobedience. The goodness of God towards men was shown, in the first instance, by the constitution of our progenitors in the state of original justice, which was to become the stable and perpetual inheritance of their posterity, if they obeyed the commandment of God. In the second instance it was shown by the concession of a mediator who should open a way of restitution to mankind after the fall. Undoubtedly the grace conferred both in the first and in the second instance was gratuitous, and therefore might have been withheld altogether, or withheld from one portion of the human race and conferred on another portion. The same is true of the angels also. But if God had selected some angels or some men from the whole multitude, by an antecedent decree, for the exclusive enjoyment of sanctifying grace and the light of glory, he must have made some other benevolent provision for the rest of the angels and of men, whom he had passed by in this decree of election. If the only benevolent provision which he determined to make for the angels and for men was the provision of a way to attain deific beatitude, then all angels and all men must have been included in this one provision. On this supposition the essential goodness of God determines him to confer celestial glory on every angel without exception, unless he sins. Likewise, in the case of Adam, the essential goodness of God determines him to confer on his posterity, without any exception, celestial glory, unless he sins or they sin.

The theory of the strict or supralapsarian Calvinists is, therefore, plainly contrary to the doctrine of the Scripture and to the dictates of reason. It denies an essential attribute of God—to wit, his goodness—and therefore subverts the total conception of God as most perfect Being. According to this theory, God willed antecedently to all foresight of sin or innocence, the salvation of the elect angels and men, and the damnation of the reprobate. For this end he decreed the obedience of the elect and the sins of the reprobate as the fit and proper means to accomplish his purpose. The sin of Adam was decreed in order to plunge all mankind into eternal ruin, and the death of Christ in order to rescue and save the elect. I do not think it necessary to say anything more about this theory. If there are any who can regard it with complacency, I give them up as beyond the reach of argument. The Synod of Dort, it is well known, rejected it, and the great majority of Calvinists, as well as the Lutherans, adopt the milder and less repulsive sublapsarian doctrine. According to this latter theory, God willed, antecedently to the foreknowledge of sin, the salvation of all angels and all men. The decree of election and reprobation, therefore, is consequent to the sin of Adam, and regards men as already lapsed into the state of original sin. All being alike unworthy of the kingdom of heaven, God may, without any derogation either to his justice or goodness, leave them as they are, without any second provision for their salvation. In his pure mercy, he chooses a certain number whom he wills to save through the Mediator whom he predestines, passing over the remainder. The Jansenists and a certain portion of the Calvinists teach that Jesus Christ died for this elect portion of mankind alone, although many other Calvinists, with the great body of Protestants, admit that he died for all men, as the Scriptures so plainly declare.

This sublapsarian doctrine is far less intolerable than the theory of the supralapsarians. It does honor to the moral sense, and to the respect for the obvious and traditional interpretation of the Scripture of those who have adopted it, that they have rejected the pure and simple Calvinistic theory, as presented in all its naked deformity. Nevertheless, the sublapsarian theory is essentially no better in itself, and contains the same skeleton under its cloak, only that it is more clumsily put together. Moderate Calvinism is what the Germans call a *Halbheit*—that is, a half-theory, the segment of a circle, or the frustum of a cone. It denies the universal benevolence of God towards the human species under one order of providence, and that order the very one specially characterized by mercy, while it affirms this benevolence in every other order, and declares that it proceeds from an essential attribute of God. Such a theory is intrinsically repugnant and self-contradictory. Either God is necessarily determined by his essential goodness to good-will toward his rational creatures, or he is not. If he is, he must have a good-will toward every rational creature without exception. If he is not, then he is indifferent toward good-will and ill-will, and therefore free to manifest the one toward a portion of his creatures, and the other toward another portion. But if God is supposed to decree good and evil to two separate classes of men, antecedently to any free acts of their own, it must be supposed that he does this because he is essentially indifferent to a benevolent or a malevolent will. It is, therefore, more consistent to suppose that all sin and consequent misery in the universe is caused by a malevolent will of God, than to suppose it in the sole case of fallen man. Moreover, this theory implies that the elect are moved toward salvation, and the reprobate toward damnation, by a necessary and irresistible impulse. And, if this is so, it is more consistent and logical to hold that the same was true of the angels and of Adam before and in the fall. The supralapsarian theory is, therefore, coherent and consistent with itself. It denies all created freedom of will, and teaches that holiness and sin, happiness and misery, are produced by the only first and efficient cause—the will of God. Those who are created for glory and beatitude are brought to their end by a necessary and irreversible law, and those who are created for ignominy and misery are made to gravitate to their doom by a similar law. The sublapsarian theory, after laying down the contrary rule as universal, proceeds to make the case of mankind after the fall an exception. Upon their theory, God is universally benevolent, yet he is malevolent toward all men except the elect. He desires the salvation of all rational creatures by an antecedent will, and decrees to give it to all, unless they forfeit it by wilful sin; yet he does not desire the salvation of the reprobate, or give them the freedom of choice by which they can refrain from sin, but dooms them before their birth to an unavoidable necessity of sinning, and to eternal torments from which he will not permit them to escape.

There is, indeed, an appearance of saving the justice and goodness of God in the statement that God does not abandon the reprobate to their doom by a decree antecedent to the foresight of sin, but subsequent to the foresight of original sin, in which all men are involved by the fall of Adam. God, it is said, wills the salvation of all men, considered as included in the first covenant made with Adam, and really provided for the salvation of all men by that covenant. But when Adam fell, the covenant was broken, mankind was ruined, and God was not obliged by his justice or goodness to provide a redemption from the effects of the fall. If in his infinite mercy he chose to rescue and save some men, in preferring these he committed no act of injustice against the others whom he passed over. This is most true, if understood in an orthodox and Catholic sense, and entirely conformed to the doctrine of Holy Scripture. But in the sense of the Lutherans, Calvinists, and Jansenists, it is most false, as an exposition of that sense will clearly show.

According to this heretical doctrine, the state of

original justice was nothing more than the natural integrity and rectitude in which God created Adam as a perfect man, with the essential and integral attributes and circumstances due to his human nature. He could not, according to his own wisdom and goodness, have created him in any different or inferior state—in any state in which his faculties were not proportioned to the attainment of the beatific vision in the kingdom of glory. By the fall he became essentially and totally evil and depraved, incapable of doing any actions or eliciting any volitions which are not sinful. All his posterity are conceived and born in this totally depraved and sinful state, and made actual sinners from the beginning of their existence, without any power to the contrary. They are consequently doomed to the fire of hell from the first instant of their conception, and compelled to do nothing while they live but add new torments to those they have inherited by generation from Adam.

This theory is irreconcilable with the doctrine of the universal good-will of God to his rational creatures. Every human soul is created immediately by God. If he creates it with a necessity of sinning, and suffering in consequence the eternal privation of all good, he has no good-will towards it, but, on the contrary, wills only the greatest possible evil to it from the very beginning of its existence.

It is a sophistical evasion, as well as a cruel mockery of the moral sense and right feelings of the human heart, to say that the unhappy soul is doomed to this hopeless misery on account of the sin of Adam imputed to it. The soul comes fresh from the creative hand of God, and by the fact of being created contracts all the essential relations of a rational creature toward the Creator. But the very act of subjecting it to such an imputation is a subversion of its most essential relation to God. It is the infliction of the greatest possible evil upon it before it has had a probation, before it has done anything to deserve punishment, before it is capable of a free moral act. It is, moreover, a contradiction in terms to assert such an imputation of the act of one individual to another individual. It cannot be done really, and a merely nominal imputation is a legal fiction, which is contrary to all justice. But the absurdity of this theory does not stop here. Total depravity destroys the moral nature, annihilates freedom of choice, and thus puts an end to the power of sinning and to all accountability. One who is incapable of doing anything else except sinning is in the category of a blind man in respect to sight, a cripple in respect to walking, an idiot in respect to rational activity. The unhappy reprobate stumbles blindly, helplessly, stupidly, down the descent of his miserable life into the open grave, and through the grave into everlasting woe, as a blind and lame idiot who had been carried up to the top of the Matterhorn might stumble over its slippery crest into the abyss beneath. It is idle to pretend to reconcile such a theory as this with the universal benevolence of God. The only consistent Calvinist is the merciless supralapsarian, who asserts only the sovereignty of God, and reduces his goodness to a mere arbitrary will of bringing the elect to glory, all the rest of the rational creation being wholly excluded from the love of God.

It is true, nevertheless, and most plainly taught in the Holy Scriptures, that the redemption of Jesus Christ is a work of pure grace and mercy. It is therefore certain that God might have left mankind unredeemed, or might have redeemed only a certain elect number. It is impossible to reconcile this doctrine of Holy Scripture with that other equally clear doctrine of the same Scripture that God loves all his creatures, on the Calvinistic theory of original justice and original sin. There must be, therefore, another and a true doctrine which is in harmony with all that the Holy Scripture teaches respecting the necessity of the divine benevolence and the gratuitousness of the divine grace. This is the Catholic doctrine—that original justice, with the annexed promise of the beatific vision, was a gratuitous and supernatural gift of God to the human race in Adam. This supernatural gift was made to depend on Adam's obedience, and was forfeited by his sin. Human nature was not totally depraved by this loss, but despoiled and changed into something worse, though still retaining all its essentials, and therefore remaining essentially good. Unquestionably, God might have carried out to the fullest extent the penalty which he had before denounced to Adam: "In the day that thou eatest thereof thou shalt surely die." He might have deprived our first parents of life immediately, and thus have destroyed the whole human race in its root. Or he might have left them on the earth to propagate their species under the changed and deteriorated conditions of the state of lapsed nature in which we are now all born, without providing a redemption and restoration through a mediator. But in this latter case he must have manifested in some way his benevolent will toward all those whom he created under these conditions, by virtue of that essential relation which all creatures bear to their Creator. The human race could not have been continued, with its history, its development through a regular series of ages, and its final consummation, without some end worthy of the wisdom and goodness of God, to which he would have conducted the race and the individuals belonging to it by his merciful providence. In point of fact, he did decree and promise a redemption; and, since it was solely and exclusively by that order of providence which is based on the redemption that he made any provision whatever for carrying out his good-will to all the posterity of Adam, they were all necessarily included in that redemption. So far as we know, our birth and existence are due merely to this decree of redemption through the Mediator. Our first parents were called to account for their sin, received their penance, were forgiven and restored to grace, with the promise of a Redeemer from the seed of the woman, before they were sent out of Paradise to begin the toils of their allotted portion of earthly life, and to beget children who should inherit a similar allotment, with its probation of labor and trial, and its annexed blessing of grace and hope through the promised Redeemer. It is therefore probable that we owe our existence and all our natural enjoyments, the green fields, the blue sky, the fresh air, and all else that is fair and pleasant, to our Lord and Saviour Jesus Christ, who has saved this world from the curse which the sin of Adam brought upon it, and from total destruction, by sprinkling upon it his precious blood.

For myself, I am firmly convinced with St. Athanasius, Suarez, and other eminent theologians, that the Incarnation of the Word was decreed before the foresight of the fall. If this be so, the universe, and especially the human race, was only created in view of, and with reference to, Christ. It is therefore on his account, and for the sake of the eternal love of the Father to him, that we received the first communication of grace in the Paradisaic state. For the same reason it was impossible that the human race should be frustrated of its supernatural end. It was the predestined race of the Incarnation, and human nature was the predestined nature of God. The Omnipotent Word could not permit his own race and his own nature to be finally ruined and destroyed. He redeemed us, therefore, because by the mere fact of our human nature we are his own blood-relations. The redemption is as wide in its extent as the relationship. But the relationship of blood to the Divine Redeemer extends to every individual of the human race, and therefore the redemption also. In a wider sense, this relationship to the Word Incarnate exists in all rational creatures, and, so far as their nature admits of it, in all created things; and in him, therefore, is the ultimate reason of their existence and motive of all the good conferred upon them by their Creator. This is taught by St. Paul in a very distinct and explicit manner in the Epistle to the Colossians: "His dear Son [the Son of his love, *Marg.*] . . . is the image of the invisible God, *the first-born of every creature:* for by him were all things created, that are in heaven, and that are in earth, visible and invisible, whether they be thrones, or dominions, or principalities, or powers: all things were created by him, *and for him:* and he is before all things, and by him all things consist. And he is the head of the body, the church: who is the beginning, the first-born from the dead; that in all things he might have the pre-eminence. For it pleased the Father that in him should all fulness dwell; and, having made peace through the blood of his cross, by him to reconcile all things unto himself; by him, I say, whether they be things in earth, or things in heaven." * St. John declares in the preface of his Gospel concerning the Word: "That was the true Light, which *lighteth every man* that cometh into the world." † St. Paul, again, in his sermon on the Hill of Mars at Athens, teaches that the supernatural and merciful providence of God embraces all men, all times and places, and all events on the earth, and connects this truth with the very idea of one God the creator of all things. "God that made the world and all things therein . . . hath made of one blood *all nations* of men for to dwell on *all the face*

* Coloss. i. 13–20.   † John i. 9.

of the earth, and hath determined the times before appointed, and the bounds of their habitation; *that they should seek the Lord*, if haply they might feel after him, and find him, though he be not far from every one of us: for in him we live, and move, and have our being; as certain also of your own poets have said, *For we are also his offspring.*" *
The same apostle, in another sermon, or rather impromptu address, to the people of Lystra, refers all common, natural blessings enjoyed by the heathen to the same source—that is, the merciful providence of God for the salvation of men: "We preach unto you that ye should turn from these vanities unto the living God, which made heaven, and earth, and the sea, and all things that are therein: who in times past suffered all nations to walk in their own ways. Nevertheless *he left not himself without witness*, in that he did good, and gave us rain from heaven, and fruitful seasons, filling our hearts with food and gladness." †

There are none, therefore, who are excluded from the decree of salvation and redemption by a decree of reprobation. Those who are deprived of the light of revelation are not on that account abandoned by God and under a necessity of sinning and incurring eternal torments. Free-will remains even in the state of fallen nature, and by it

* Acts xvii. 24-28.   † Acts xiv. 15-17.

the heathen are able to perform acts of natural virtue. They have a natural law, as St. Paul teaches in the Epistle to the Romans: "For when the Gentiles, which have not the law, do by nature the things contained in the law, these, having not the law, are a law unto themselves: which show the work of *the law written in their hearts*, their conscience also bearing witness, and their thoughts the meanwhile accusing or else excusing one another."* It is not my purpose to discuss more particularly the questions which relate to the condition of those who are out of the ordinary way of salvation without any fault of their own, or who die in the state of original sin only, without any actual sin. I have proved clearly enough from the Scriptures and from general principles that no rational creature can be excluded from the merciful providence and good-will of God, except by his own free and voluntary act. All those, therefore, who are deprived of the opportunity of receiving the grace of regeneration in Christ, and attaining the kingdom of heaven, are in some way provided for by the goodness and mercy of God. No argument can be derived from their case against the universal operation of the divine benevolence. Nor is there any valid objection furnished by it against the doctrine that God decreed to provide in Christ a

---

* Rom. ii. 14, 15.

redemption universal in its extension for the human race. There is no human being, adult or infant, who is excluded from the grace of regeneration and eternal salvation by any decree of antecedent reprobation. Those who fail of it without their own fault fail through the operation of second causes. Each and every one of them is as capable of receiving the divine grace, in case it were applied to him, as any of those who are actually regenerated. All men are generated in the initial and inchoate order of grace and salvation, because redemption is generic and not individual, and the Redeemer promised to our first parents becomes *ipso facto* the Redeemer of the entire human race. Therefore every one to whom the way of salvation is proposed can be certain that this way is open to him, and that there is no hidden decree of reprobation recorded against him which renders him incapable of receiving or persevering in grace and obtaining heaven. This has been amply proved from the Holy Scriptures. There are, however, a few obscure and difficult passages in the Scriptures which appear to those who have been used to read the Bible through Calvinistic spectacles to have a very dark and terrifying aspect, and to overshadow some part of the human race with the gloomy cloud of reprobation. I will therefore examine these passages, and explain their true sense before proceeding further.

The first of these passages occurs in what is called the Protevangelium, or Primary Gospel, recorded by Moses in the third chapter of Genesis: "I will put enmity between thee and the woman, and between *thy seed* and her seed."* What is the seed of the serpent? Evidently not a distinct race of human demons generated by the devil. It is the multitude of the wicked, in whom the likeness of the devil is formed by their voluntary reception of, and obedience to, the false principles and maxims which he suggests to them. Here again the American Bible Society furnishes a number of most satisfactory references to other texts, which explain the meaning of this one in accordance with the orthodox sense of the church: " But when he saw many of the Pharisees and Sadducees come to his baptism, he said unto them, *O generation of vipers*, who hath warned you to flee from the wrath to come?" "He answered and said unto them, He that soweth the good seed is the Son of man; the field is the world; the good seed are the children of the kingdom; but the tares are the children of the wicked one; *the enemy that sowed them is the devil.*" " Woe unto you, Scribes and Pharisees, *hypocrites!* . . . *Ye serpents*, ye generation of vipers, how can ye escape the damnation of hell?" " Jesus answered them, Verily, verily, I say unto

---

*Gen. iii. 15.

you, Whosoever committeth sin is the servant of sin. . . . If ye were Abraham's children, ye would do the works of Abraham. But now ye seek to kill me, a man that hath told you the truth. . . . Ye do the deeds of your father. . . . *Ye are of your father the devil*, and the lusts of your father ye will do. He was a murderer from the beginning, and abode not in the truth, because there is no truth in him." " But Elymas the sorcerer [a chief one among the spiritists of those days] witnstood them, seeking to turn away the deputy from the faith. Then Saul, filled with the Holy Ghost, set his eyes on him, and said, O full of all subtilty and all mischief, *thou child of the devil*, thou enemy of all righteousness, wilt thou not cease to pervert the right ways of the Lord?" "*He that committeth sin is of the devil.*" * This last text sums up and explains the whole series. A man becomes a child of the devil, or one of the seed of the old serpent, by sinning. I will prove hereafter that some of these, and even the worst of them, are apostates from grace and from faith, who have been once justified and sanctified, and for whom Christ is expressly declared to have shed his blood. It has already been proved that God desires their conversion and invites them to repentance. It is

---

* Matt. iii. 7, xiii. 37, and xxiii. 33 ; John viii. 34 ; Acts xiii. 8 ; 1 John iii. 8, with the several contexts.

therefore purely their own free act which makes them children of the devil, and not a sentence of reprobation under which they are born.

The second difficulty is found in the case of Esau and Jacob, cited by St. Paul in the ninth chapter of the Epistle to the Romans: "When Rebecca also had conceived by one, even by our father Isaac (for the children being not yet born, neither having done any good or evil, that the purpose of God according to election might stand, not of works, but of him that calleth), it was said unto her, The elder shall serve the younger." So far as the election of Jacob and the rejection of Esau are considered in reference to their own persons, it is evident from the very words quoted and from the entire narrative of Genesis that these relate to merely temporal matters. Esau, although the first-born of the twins, was put aside, and Jacob preferred to the dignity of patriarch of the chosen people. St. Paul declares that this was done, not on account of any worthiness in Jacob or unworthiness in Esau, but according to the sovereign will of God. And when, in another place (Heb. xii. 17)—a passage often cited to prove that some persons cannot repent if they try ever so much—the apostle says that 'when he would have inherited the blessing, he was rejected: for he found no place of repentance, though he sought it carefully with tears," it is plainly the blessing of the birthright that is exclusively referred to, and not the forgiveness of sin. The passage from Malachy which St. Paul proceeds to quote in the Epistle to the Romans, "Jacob have I loved, but Esau have I hated," will be seen by any one who will read the prophecy to refer to the difference of God's dealings with the Jews and Idumæans. The former were restored to their own land, after they had been sent into captivity for their sins, by an act of grace and mercy. The latter were exterminated, on account of their sins, by an act of justice. "Jacob have I loved" means, therefore, Jacob's posterity have I treated with special mercy; "Esau have I hated" means, Esau's posterity I have treated with a just severity. When the apostle, then, asks the question in the person of an objector, "Is there unrighteousness with God?" the sense of it is: When two classes of persons or two individuals have equally sinned, and equally deserve punishment, is it unjust for God to be more merciful to the one than to the other? "God forbid. For he saith to Moses, I will have mercy on whom I will have mercy, and I will have compassion on whom I will have compassion." This was said to Moses when he asked for a special manifestation of the presence of God with the children of Israel, and desired to see his glory. His request was so far granted that God gave him some kind of a supernatural vision of his goodness. It evidently means that God bestows his gratuitous and supernatural graces according to his own will, and that man has no power to deserve or attain them by his own natural qualities or efforts. This is the deduction made by the apostle: "So then it is not of him that willeth, nor of him that runneth, but of God that showeth mercy." All this forms a part of St. Paul's argument on the general thesis of his Epistle. This thesis is: that vocation to the faith and justification were given both to the Jews and the Gentiles, gratuitously, and for the sake of Jesus Christ, and were not merited by any natural descent from Abraham and outward observance of the Mosaic Law, or by any observance of the natural law.

A third difficulty follows immediately upon the second, in the instance of Pharaoh. "For the Scripture saith unto Pharaoh, Even for this same purpose have I raised thee up, that I might show my power in thee, and that my name might be declared throughout all the earth. Therefore hath he mercy on whom he will, and whom he will he hardeneth." It is not said that God *created* Pharaoh to show his power by drowning him in the Red Sea, but that he "raised him up," or, as other versions have it, constituted, placed, or preserved him. God willed that Pharaoh should listen to Moses, embrace the true religion, obey his commandments, and attain salvation. By his own wilful pride and obstinacy, he turned all the temporal and spiritual advantages which were given him for his own good into the occasion of his own signal destruction. Moses says expressly that he hardened his own heart. After he had hardened his own heart, God hardened him still more. That is, God, foreknowing that he would be further hardened by reason of the obstinacy which he had caused in himself, by a certain course of his providence toward him, and would madly oppose himself to his will, pursued that very course toward him, and gave him the opportunity of carrying out the purposes of his proud will, until he rushed upon the punishment and ruin which He had prepared for him. St. Paul gives this as an instance under a general law of divine providence. "Whom he will he hardeneth." Some persons who have provoked the indignation of the Almighty are placed in circumstances which allow them the opportunity of sinning with a high hand, and of going on in a successful and prosperous career of crime. He does not interfere to prevent efficaciously their arriving at an obdurate and final impenitence, either by giving them a continuous series of special graces, or by thwarting their undertakings. And, at last, he makes them terrible examples of his justice and severity. "He hath mercy on whom he will." Other persons, equally or more undeserving, are checked and stopped in their career of sin, and in many instances become eminent saints and servants of God.

Still another of these difficulties occurs in the very answer which the apostle makes to an objection against his statement respecting the case of Pharaoh: "Thou wilt say then unto me, Why doth he yet find fault? for who hath resisted his will? Nay but, O man, who art thou that repliest against God? Shall the thing formed say to him that formed it, Why hast thou made me thus? Hath not the potter power over the clay, of the same lump to make one vessel unto honor, and another unto dishonor?" The explanation of this passage depends entirely on the understanding of the point of comparison between mankind and clay. It is not, as wholly inert and passive under the potter's hand, that clay is an apt figure of sinful men under the controlling power of God's providence, and this is not, therefore, the point of the comparison. The want of any determining force in the clay by which it can naturally become a vessel of honor is that to which St. Paul compares the lack of natural and positive aptitude to sanctity and glory in man. God alone can fashion human nature into his own similitude in glory. This he does, in the case of "the vessels of mercy which he had afore prepared unto glory," but not without their free co-operation with grace, since, as the apostle strongly insists in this and other chapters of the Epistle, these vessels of mercy were those from among both Jews and Gentiles who believed in Jesus Christ and thus obtained "the righteousness which is of faith." So, also, the vessels made "unto dishonor" are expressly declared by the apostle to have incurred this ignominy through their unbelief, "for they stumbled at that stumbling-stone"—that is, refused to receive their true Messias on account of his humility and the requisition he made on them to give up their national pride and prejudices. The apostle therefore continues, immediately after the principal passage above quoted: "What if God, willing to show his wrath, and to make his power known, *endured with much long-suffering* the vessels of wrath *fitted to destruction?*" How, and by whom, fitted to destruction? By themselves, through their sins and their resistance to grace, by which they have given themselves that hardness which renders them unfit to be fashioned into vessels of honor. That God spares their lives, and gives them the means and opportunities which they abuse, is in itself an act of mercy. That he turns their wicked projects and criminal acts into an indirect occasion of the manifestation of his own power and glory through their destruction, is an act of justice. St. Paul's objector impiously accuses the justice of God, because he condemns persons and acts which he has turned by his power into instruments of accomplishing his own infallible decrees. For example, the treason of Judas, the unbelief and malice of the Jewish rulers, the cowardice and injustice of Pilate, by means of which was accomplished the crucifixion of the Lord, who thereby redeemed the world. The reply of St. Paul to this objection is an application of the fundamental principle of the sovereignty of God over his creatures, illustrated by the power of the potter over clay. The potter cannot make anything essentially impossible or essentially different from the nature of clay out of clay. He is bound by the laws of nature and the rules of art. Neither can God exercise his sovereign power in contravention of the essential attributes of his own being, which are as necessary laws or regulating principles of his operation, or in contravention of the rules of his divine art, which are moral and in harmony with the freedom of the human will. He cannot, therefore, make a vessel of dishonor out of any one who has not voluntarily made himself fit for nothing else than ignominy and destruction. But, if one has prepared himself for this ignominious destination, it is the sovereign right of God to bring good out of the evil which he has wrought, and out of his destruction which is the just recompense for it, by making both the occasion of manifesting his own power and glory.

This last act of God proceeds, therefore, from his will as consequent upon the foresight of sin and final impenitence, and not from his antecedent will. For this reason, the apostle, speaking of the time during which the probation of the sinner lasts, declares that God endures him with much long-suffering, implying, what is elsewhere in the Scripture distinctly taught, that he is waiting for his repentance. It is, therefore, altogether the fault of those who are made vessels of dishonor that they are not made vessels of honor, and not because they are previously destined to dishonor. And St. Paul distinctly teaches this in another place, where he uses the very same figure. " But in a great house there are not only vessels of gold and of silver, but also of wood and of earth; and some to honor, and some to dishonor. *If a man therefore purge himself from these* [sins], he shall be a vessel unto honor, sanctified, and meet for the master's use, and prepared unto every good work."*

There is still one more favorite proof-text, taken by Calvinists from St. Peter, which requires to be noticed. " The stone which the builders disallowed, the same is made the head of the corner, and a stone of stumbling, and a rock of offence, even to them which stumble at the word, being disobedient: *whereunto also they were appointed.*"† This text is easily explained in conformity with the true

---

* 2 Tim. ii. 21.   † 1 Peter ii. 7, 8.

doctrine of the Holy Scriptures as teaching, not that unbelievers are appointed or predestined to unbelief in order that they may be ruined, but that they are appointed to stumble over that stone which they have despised and rejected, as a punishment of their unbelief. "Whosoever shall fall on this stone shall be broken; but on whomsoever it shall fall, it will grind him to powder."

All these passages which appear to contain a difficulty, and, as taken singly, are plausibly interpreted in their own sense by those who bring to the reading of the Scripture a preconceived Calvinistic theory, must be understood in a sense which harmonizes with all the rest of the Scripture. Obscure passages must be interpreted by those which are perfectly plain. Ambiguous passages must be interpreted in a sense consonant to reason, natural theology, and the analogy of faith. It is hardly necessary to insist on the greater conformity to reason, natural theology, and the analogy of faith, of the interpretation here given. I have also quoted other passages of Scripture which are clear and easily intelligible, in which a criterion for determining this interpretation as the only true one is furnished. I will add one more from St. James, which may be taken as the summing up of the whole case, and is the more significant since this apostle probably had the express intention of condemning the false interpretation placed by heretics on some passages in St. Paul's Epistle: "Let no man say when he is tempted, I am tempted of God; for God cannot be tempted with evil, neither tempteth he any man."* The phrase translated "God cannot be tempted with evil (or evils)" is ambiguous in the Greek, and is rendered by St. Jerome *intentator malorum est—i.e.*, is not a tempter of evils, instead of *intentabilis*, or untemptable. This last rendering, which is the same with that of King James's Version, is followed by Kenrick, who, with his usual exquisite and concise wisdom, explains it thus: "God is not tempted to evil, and consequently does not tempt others. To solicit others to sin implies personal corruption." That is to say: God, as infinitely good and holy, cannot possibly will any evil, or find anything pleasing to himself in the evil of his creatures. Consequently, he cannot become in any way the author of sin, or create any rational being for sin and evil. Nothing but good proceeds from his antecedent will, and, by his consequent will, he can only permit sin as the free act of a creature, and inflict evil on him as the just and necessary consequence of his sin. And then the apostle goes on to say: "Do not err, my beloved brethren [by referring evil to the antecedent will of God, because no evil proceeds from it]. Every *good gift* and every perfect gift is from above,

---

* St. James i. 13.

and cometh down from the Father of lights, with whom is no variableness, neither shadow of turning"; and who cannot, therefore, have two contrary wills towards his creatures — a benevolent will towards some, and a malevolent will towards others.

The grand fundamental doctrine of the Holy Scriptures being therefore established on an impregnable foundation, that God wills the salvation of the human race as such, and that Jesus Christ died to redeem the race, we are prepared to consider more closely the nature of the way of salvation revealed by the Gospel. All that theory of salvation which is built on the false assumption that our Lord died for the elect only, and which cannot subsist without it, is at once swept away. The theory, namely, that the obedience and death of the Lord contains in itself everything necessary to secure the salvation of each individual who is redeemed, is proved to be false. It is admitted and maintained by all orthodox Protestants, that all men are born in original sin, saving certain exceptional cases, and that a very large number of the human race live and die in actual sin, which is never remitted either in this world or in the world to come; that is, a large part of mankind are not saved. But as Christ died for all men, and therefore for those who are not saved, it follows that the salvation of any individual does not follow necessarily from the fact that Christ died for him, and that the race has been redeemed. But, if our Lord, by his obedience and death, and by his personal merit, fulfilled everything necessary to the justification and salvation of the men for whom he died, every one of these must infallibly be saved. It is evident, therefore, that something else is necessary to the salvation of an individual beside the mere fact of his being included in that multitude for whom the Lord offered up the sacrifice of his life. That the obedience of Jesus Christ unto death, even the death of the cross, is the only meritorious cause of redemption, remission of sins, and justification, is indisputable. But it is equally evident that other causes, subordinate to this, must concur with it to actual justification and salvation. That all men have been redeemed and saved by Jesus Christ, as has been already proved, must therefore mean, in the first instance, and irrespective of any further conditions, only this: that all men have been placed in a condition in which salvation is possible. Original and actual sin have been made remissible to the whole human race, and every individual included in it. Every human being as such, as a child of Adam and a member of the human race, is a fit and capable subject of the grace of regeneration, whose proper term is eternal life.

But there are certain conditions to be verified in each particular case; there is a certain way of salvation on which each one must enter, in order that the redemption of the cross may be made effectual to his actual deliverance from sin and its penalty, whether original or actual.

What these conditions really are I shall proceed to prove from the Holy Scripture, taking for granted, however, all that is admitted and maintained by those whom I am specially addressing. Some of these conditions depend on the action of God, others on the operation of second causes, and still others on the free acts of individuals. In the case of all those to whom the way of salvation is clearly and distinctly proposed, it is plain from what has been already proved that their salvation is conditioned only on their own free choice and action. It is certain that God wills their salvation, and that Jesus Christ has died in order to merit and obtain salvation for them. By the very supposition, there is no operation of second causes hindering the saving will of God from taking effect upon them, unless they place the obstacle themselves. For they are supposed to know, or to have the power of knowing, what the way of salvation is. Whatever depends on God is certain to be done for them; for he who wills the end wills the means, and therefore God, who wills the end—eternal salvation—will furnish sufficient means, so far as these depend on him, if they do, on their part, what they are able and bound to do. I do not propose to consider at all the case of those who are deprived of the ordinary means of regeneration, or who are in invincible ignorance of the way of salvation, through the operation of second causes independent of their own will. An explanation of the providence of God toward such persons, and the reconciliation of the difficulties presented by it with the doctrine of the Scripture that Christ died in obedience to the will of the Father for the salvation of all men, must be sought elsewhere. My purpose is to explain to those who will read this book; and who already believe that salvation is of the free grace of God, through the merits of the Mediator, Jesus Christ, both God and man; what is the full and complete way of salvation through Christ. All that I have heretofore proved has been proved with reference to its special application to their own individual case. I have wished to convince them, in the first place, that they are without doubt included in the saving will of God, and in the intention for which the Lord and Saviour of mankind sacrificed himself on the cross. In the second place, that there are other requisites, besides their redemption by the cross, to their actual salvation. In the third place, that some of these requisites or conditions depend on their own free will. And, in the fourth place, that when they once know and desire to enter upon the true way of salvation, all that is requisite on the part of God will certainly be supplied, if they fulfil what is requisite on their part by a right use of their free will. In fine, their salvation depends on themselves, and is fully in their own power. They have only to seek sincerely to find the way of salvation, and when they have found it, to walk in it perseveringly, and they are sure to obtain salvation from God, whose will is that they may be saved, who has provided salvation for them in Jesus Christ, and who will infallibly accomplish in them his own saving will, by giving them grace, and bringing them finally to glory and beatitude.

I have now to begin the task of explaining from the Holy Scriptures what are those requisites and conditions which constitute the way of salvation through Jesus Christ. I will take them up one by one in regular order, beginning with faith as the first requisite to justification, which will be considered in the next chapter.

CHAPTER SECOND.

Justification by Faith—The Lutheran and Calvinistic Doctrine of Justification by Faith alone refuted—The Nature and Office of Faith as the first Prerequisite to Justification explained—Statement and Proof of the Catholic Doctrine concerning Saving Faith.

THAT man is "justified by faith" is a theological axiom. But even axioms are worthless unless their terms are clearly defined. It is therefore absolutely necessary to define the true sense and meaning of the term faith as it is used in the Holy Scripture. I will first state the definition, and afterwards prove from Scripture that it is the true and correct definition. Faith is that act by which the intellect, aided by grace, firmly assents to the truth which God reveals, because he reveals it.

The most essential part of this definition, so far as my present purpose is concerned, is that which fixes upon faith the sense of belief in truth revealed by God. It is obvious enough that it is commonly used in this sense. The objective matter which terminates the act of believing is called "The Faith." One who elicits an act of faith is said to believe. Throughout the New Testament, as well as in all common Christian parlance, these terms are used as correlative. This fact is by itself sufficient to fix the technical sense of the term faith, when it denotes the first essential prerequisite and condition of justification. Whoever asserts that it has another sense, is loaded with the whole burden of proof. Until the Calvinist adduces clear proof from the Scripture that justifying faith is something distinct from belief in revealed truth, he is entitled to no attention, we are not bound to refute him, nor are we bound to give any other reason for our own definition, beyond the common and ordinary acceptation of terms in the inspired and uninspired documents of the Christian religion.

Nevertheless, as we write for the sake of instructing enquirers after truth, and not merely for confuting or silencing its adversaries, we will give our candid readers a clear exposition of the nature of justifying faith, from the Scripture itself, and in the language of the inspired apostles of Christ.

The most splendid description of the divine excellence and effects of faith ever couched in the poor language of men, is to be found in the Epistle to the Hebrews. It is the theme of this most sublime of all the compositions of St. Paul, from the beginning to the end, and I earnestly exhort every reader who wishes to understand fully the argument of this chapter to read it through attentively and at once, in order that he may see the connection of thought and reasoning between its various parts, and grasp its general idea. The apostle begins by declaring that God " has in these last days spoken to us by his Son." The author and the medium of divine revelation are here presented, with the implication that the revelation which was inchoate and imperfect under the Old Law, has been consummated and completed by Jesus Christ. The apostle begins the second chapter by the practical inference that "therefore we ought to give the more earnest heed to the things which we have heard"; and in the third chapter warns the Hebrew Christians not to imitate the example of their fathers, who were shut out of the promised land, and " could not enter in because of unbelief." Continuing the same subject in the fourth chapter, he says that " the word preached did not profit them, not being mixed with faith in them that heard it," and concludes with this exhortation: " Seeing then that we have a great highpriest, that is passed into the heavens, Jesus the Son of God, let us *hold fast our profession.*"

After reproaching them with their dulness and weakness of faith, by reason of which, he tells them at the end of the fifth chapter, " ye have need that one teach you again which be the first principles of the oracles of God," he exhorts them, in the sixth, to "be not slothful, but followers of them who through faith and patience inherit the promises." In this connection he brings out the ground of the infallible certitude of faith, which is the veracity of God and the clearness of the revelation which he has made of the truths believed by the faithful. "God, willing more abundantly to show unto the heirs of promise the immutability of his counsel, confirmed it by an oath: that by two immutable things in which it was impossible for God to lie, we might have a strong consolation." In the tenth chapter he makes another exhortation to firm faith in the divine truths, chiefly relating to the Incarnation and Redemption, which he has been continually developing from the beginning of the Epistle. "Let us draw near with a true heart in full assurance of faith. . . . Let us hold fast the profession of our faith without wavering. . . . Now the just shall live by faith; but if any man draw back, my soul shall have no pleasure in him. But we are not of them who draw back unto perdition, but of them that *believe to the saving of the soul.*"

The teaching of St. Paul concerning faith culminates in the eleventh chapter, which he begins by a descriptive definition of faith. "Now faith is the substance of things hoped for, the evidence of things not seen." This translation is as good and literal a rendering as we can have of the Greek, and agrees closely with the Latin. The idea presented is perfectly clear—viz., that faith is that light which gives the human intellect a certain, subjective apprehension of the objective realities of the supernatural order. In plainer language, faith makes real to the mind of man the revealed truths and mysteries of God. To borrow Dr. Newman's expression, it is a "real assent" to truths about divine things which are either dimly visible or totally invisible to the naked eye of reason. I have, therefore, demonstrated the truth and correctness of the definition which I gave of faith at the beginning of this chapter—a definition which is essentially the same with that given by St. Paul, differing from it only in its substitution of scientific for descriptive terms.

The apostle goes on to say that "through faith we understand that the worlds were framed by the word of God, so that things which are seen were not made of things which do appear." This is an illustration of the definition already given. Faith is belief in revealed truth, and one of the first doctrines of revealed truth is the creation of the world out of nothing by the power of God. The apostle then cites Abel as an example of faith, evidently because of the profession which he made of his belief in the Redeemer to come, through his bloody sacrifice. He next cites Enoch, and gives an indirect and inferential proof of his faith, which furnishes us with another most clear and irrefragable evidence of the real nature of faith, as well as with a succinct statement of its formal object. He proves that Enoch had faith, from the testimony of Scripture that he pleased God. "But without faith it is impossible to please him: for he that cometh to God *must believe that he is, and that he is a rewarder of them that diligently seek him.*" The brilliant constellation of martyrs, prophets, and saints to whom St. Paul directs our gaze in language of unequalled eloquence throughout the whole of this chapter, are examples of the same firm belief in the word and truth of God, revealing to them the supernatural blessings contained in the Incarnation, Redemption, and Resurrection of the Son of God, and in the divine economy of grace. The twelfth chapter is an application of the lessons taught by the faith of the fathers to their children, the Hebrew Christians, and it winds up by the exhortation: "See that ye refuse not him that speaketh: for if they escaped not who refused him that spake on earth, much more shall not we escape, if we turn away from him that speaketh from heaven."

I have already quoted enough from the doctrinal teaching of St. Paul to fully answer my purpose. But I will add one more passage equally full and strong from another Epistle. In the tenth chapter of the Epistle to the Roman Church, the apostle expressly describes that faith which is the root and ground of true justification, as distinguished from the pretended justice which is based on a mere outward observance of Jewish rites, or on purely natural virtue. "The righteousness which is of faith speaketh on this wise, Say not in thine heart, Who shall ascend into heaven? etc. But what saith it? The word is nigh thee, even in thy mouth, and in thy heart: *that is, the word of faith, which we preach;* that if thou shalt *confess with thy mouth the Lord Jesus,* and shalt *believe in thine heart that God hath raised him from the dead,* thou shalt be saved. For with the heart man believeth unto righteousness; and with the mouth confession is made unto salvation." Evidently, the faith from which springs this righteousness and justification is a belief in the message of God given through Christ and the apostles, the outward manifestation of which is a public confession of the creed or faith of the apostles.

It is plain from this definition of the essence and nature of faith that it is not alone and separate from other prerequisites and conditions sufficient to justification. It is impossible to maintain the heresy of justification by faith alone without completely altering the notion of faith which is given by the teaching of Holy Scripture. The false notion of faith and justification invented by Luther and supported by a gross falsification of the text of St. Paul in his German translation, but more logically elaborated by Calvin, is based on the doctrine that Christ died for the elect only, their sins being imputed to him, and his righteousness imputed to them. According to this heretical doctrine, justifying faith is a belief infused by the Holy Spirit into the soul of an elect person that Christ died for him, and that as a necessary consequence his sins are remitted, and a right to eternal life is conveyed to him, once for all, without any need of anything further being done in order to the completeness of his justification, or any danger that he may ever lose it. The very groundwork of this gross and deadly heresy has been completely removed in our first chapter. In that, I have proved that Christ died for all men. No one can infer, therefore, from the certitude of his belief that Christ died for him as one of the human race, that his sins are remitted; that he is justified; that he is predestined; or that he will be finally saved. Faith teaches each one who believes the way of salvation, gives him the motive of working out his salvation, and furnishes him with a supernatural principle of activity, a disposition for receiving the grace which justifies, a light and impulse to direct and stimulate him in corresponding with grace; but does not of itself justify a sinner. One who thinks and judges candidly and sincerely must necessarily admit this conclusion. I have proved beyond a cavil that faith is belief in the truth revealed by Jesus Christ, and proposed by him to all men. The summary of this truth is the creed of the apostles, as all Christians admit. No one can pretend that a man is justified and rendered secure of salvation by simply believing the Apostles' Creed. The belief and confession of the Christian and Catholic faith, which is briefly summarized in this creed, is a condition *sine quâ non* to salvation, but not the sole condition. The man who believes in his heart and confesses with his mouth the faith of Jesus Christ will be saved, if he acts in a manner consistent with his profession, if he carries out his faith into obedience to the law of Christ, but not otherwise. This is obvious and certain, and no person capable of reasoning can dispute it with a good conscience. But I will nevertheless prove it in an explicit manner from the Scripture.

Those who have a strong faith, but weak virtue, frequently fall into the practical error of trusting to their faith as a substitute for good works. It seems that some persons of that sort took advantage of certain expressions in the Epistles of St. Paul to avow boldly in the form of a false doctrine this fatal practical delusion of all times. St. James of Jeru salem wrote his Epistle chiefly for the purpose of condemning this perversion of St. Paul's doctrine, and of making a more explicit and clear statement of the relation between faith and works than that which St. Paul had been called on, by the nature of the topics concerning which he was treating, to set forth. The following is the language which he uses, so plain and unmistakable, that although the malice and sophistry of heresy have wrested and perverted it like everything else in Scripture, the blunt, audacious common sense of Luther would not permit him to see in it anything but a direct opposite to his own doctrine of justification by faith alone; wherefore he rejected the whole Epistle from his self-made canon.

"What doth it profit, my brethren, though a man say he hath faith, and have not works? *can faith save him?* . . . Faith, if it have not works, is dead, *being alone*. Thou believest that there is one God; thou doest well: the devils also believe and tremble. But wilt thou know, O vain man, that faith without works is dead? . . . . You see then how that by works a man is justified, and not by faith only. . . . For as the body without the spirit is dead, so faith without works is dead also." *

* St. James ii. 14–26.

St. James is undoubtedly here using the word faith in the sense of the definition I have already given—of belief in divine truth. But, although his direct and immediate object is to prove that a man is not justified by a sound and orthodox belief alone, the proof is equally conclusive against the doctrine of justification by faith alone, taken in any sense which separates it from obedience to the law of God. For he expressly teaches " that by works a man is justified," and therefore, let faith be what it may—trust in the merits of Christ, confidence in the mercy of God, a conviction that one is in the state of grace, hope of the forgiveness of sins and final salvation, or any other form of personal and individual application to one's self of the promises of God—it remains as a truth taught by inspiration in the Scripture, that a man is justified by works, and that nothing is sufficient to justify him which is separate from the inward, operative principle which produces good works. Any assertion that faith alone justifies is therefore directly in the teeth of St. James's declaration.

It is true that some persons explain faith in such a way as to make it include both hope and charity, and assert justification by faith alone in that sense. But these persons really do not hold any doctrine essentially different from the Catholic doctrine on this point. They mean by faith a complex principle, which is called in Catholic language *fides formata*—that is, faith informed or animated by the love of God, and actually operative in obedience to the divine law. In this sense faith is the adequate and complete inward principle of justification and of sanctification. It alone justifies, as distinguished from every other species of righteousness, or holiness, or virtue, or reason of any kind for claiming the favor of God and the approbation of conscience, which does not proceed from faith as its root. But this is a wide and improper sense in which faith is taken, and not the strict and proper sense. Strictly speaking, faith is distinct from hope and charity, even in the justified man, although not separated from them. "Now abideth these three, faith, hope, and charity; but the greatest of these is charity."* Christian hope and charity cannot exist without faith, from which they proceed. But faith can subsist without either hope or charity, and hope can subsist without charity. The quality which makes hope a fit disposition to justification is received from faith, and the same is true of charity. We are therefore justified by faith in this sense: that faith, joined with the other prerequisites, disposes the soul for justification, and that faith is the root and principle of those other

---

* 1 Cor. xiii. 13.

prerequisites—viz., hope and charity. This is the doctrine of the Council of Trent, which explains justification by faith as follows: "When, therefore, the apostle says that man is justified by faith and gratuitously, these words are to be understood in this sense, which the perpetual consent of the Catholic Church has held and expressed, to wit, that we are said to be justified by faith for this reason: because faith is the beginning of human salvation, the foundation and root of all justification, without which it is impossible to please God, and attain to the fellowship of his children; but we are said to be justified gratuitously because none of those things which precede justification, whether faith or works, merit the grace itself of justification." *

In the light of this explanation of the true sense of St. Paul and of the other inspired writers, all the difficulties which beset certain parts of the apostle's teaching vanish like mists before the sun. Any person who will apply this key to the Epistles of St. Paul, in which he places the righteousness which is of faith in opposition to that which is by the works of the law, will unlock all their perplexities, and perceive the perfect agreement between St. Paul and St. James. St. Paul proves, in opposition to the Jews, that the works of the law—circumci-

* Sess. vi. c. 8.

sion, sacrifice, the observance of rites and ceremonies, and the worship of one God—have no intrinsic power or efficacy, as separated from the merit of the obedience and death of Christ, to justify a sinner. But he does not teach that, when performed in the spirit of faith, they were not, through the merits of Christ, the appointed means and conditions of obtaining justification through the grace of God so long as the law continued in force. He proves that the philosophical virtues of the heathen had no intrinsic force of justification. But he does not teach that these purely natural virtues were not a negative preparation for the grace of faith, or that those who had faith under the law of nature were not justified by the merits of Christ, through the means of a compliance with the dictates of the natural law written in their hearts. He teaches that those who have received the law of Christ do not merit the grace of justification by any works which they do before they are justified. But he does not teach that these works, performed in the spirit of faith and obedience, are not the essential prerequisites and conditions of obtaining a free justification through the merits of Christ. This is the only point under discussion at present. It is agreed on both sides that salvation is a gratuitous work, or grace of God toward men; that the sins of those men who are justified, whether original or actual, are forgiven on account of the expiation which Jesus Christ has accomplished on the cross; and that grace, justification, and salvation are granted to all those who are saved, on account of the merits of Christ. The only question is, respecting the conditions or prerequisites by which an individual is disposed and made fit to receive justifying grace, and the instrumental causes or means by which this grace is actually communicated to him. The first of these is faith, which I have proved to be a firm belief in the revelation which God has made. I have also proved that other acts, operations, or works of the mind and will of man, under the exciting influence of divine grace, are necessary to perfect and complete faith. And I shall now proceed to prove from the Holy Scriptures of the New Testament, and especially from the Epistles of St. Paul, what are these other prerequisites and instrumental causes of justification.

CHAPTER THIRD.

Other Prerequisites of Justification—Repentance and Conversion to God—The Formal Cause and the Instruments of Justification—Regeneration and Sanctifying Grace—The Sacraments Instruments of Grace—Baptism the Sacrament of Regeneration.

THE Calvinistic heresy leaves intact the great articles of the Creed and of the Catholic faith which are immediately related to God and our Lord Jesus Christ. But it subverts from the foundation all that part of the faith which relates to the divine operation of the Mediator through secondary causes and instruments, by which he effects the regeneration and exaltation of the race which he has redeemed. In regard to all this portion of the system of Christianity, it is the most radical of heresies, because it denies the very principle on which it is based, and substitutes another which is totally opposite and contrary. This false principle is the doctrine which I have already refuted—that man is justified by faith alone. The Calvinist constructs this doctrine from certain perverted and misinterpreted texts of Scripture, with which he forms by his own private judgment, or rather, in most cases, by a blind following of the private judgment of his unauthorized teachers, a system of his own, which to certain minds is the most captivating of all errors, partly on account of its logical coherence and completeness, and partly on account of the perfect security and assurance of salvation on easy terms with which it dazzles and deludes its victims. The man who fancies that a certain feeling or state of his soul, which he calls faith, justifies him at once, completely, and for ever, giving him a sure sign that he has been absolutely predestined and elected to salvation, freeing him in an instant from the imputation of all past and future sin, and clothing him with a spotless robe of righteousness, which he is equally incapable of staining by guilt or making more brilliant by merit, naturally and logically concludes that he has no need of anything else, and cannot profit by anything whatever, whether in heaven or on the earth. He needs no teacher, no priest, no intercessor, no sacraments, no church. Faith gives him everything; and even his peccadilloes or his more grievous delinquencies give him no just occasion for alarm or anxiety. So long as the mind of a man is possessed by this persuasion or conviction, he cannot be reached by argument, or even induced to pay attention to, much less examine, the grounds and reasons on which the Catholic doctrine presents its claim to a hearing. Of what use is it for a man who already possesses the secret of the king to listen to men who offer to explain to him the royal will and intention, or the way of gaining the royal favor, even if they profess to be his ministers? A firm and decided Calvinist will not even pay attention to the inspired apostles themselves, or give heed to the plain teachings of the Holy Scripture. His chosen texts are the pith and marrow of Scripture for him. Upon these he dwells; they are for him, as it were, in large capitals; the rest is glided over, or glossed and twisted into forced conformity with his perverted sense of isolated texts.

But I beg leave to represent to those who are conscientious and reasonable, even though they have imbibed Calvinistic doctrines from their early teaching, that this course is wrong and inconsistent. One who professes to believe that "all Scripture is given by inspiration of God, and is profitable for doctrine," is bound to pay as much reverence to one portion of it as to another. One who believes that it is his duty to read and examine it for himself is bound to consider, compare, and weigh all its doctrinal statements, and to interpret them in such a manner that they will be consistent and harmonious with each other. I am about to cite a number of these passages which cannot possibly be reconciled with the Calvinistic interpretation of the texts in which the office of faith in justification is set forth. They are utterly contradictory to every possible interpretation of the Scripture teaching respecting faith and justification; except the one which I have proposed. And therefore, although I have proved sufficiently the Catholic doctrine, so far as I have gone, in the preceding chapters, the proofs I am now going to adduce are a distinct and independent demonstration of the same, as well as an additional evidence of the truth in respect to new points not yet discussed. These proofs begin at the point already reached—viz., that the sinner makes the first step toward obtaining remission and grace by believing the word of God which is preached to him by Jesus Christ and his appointed ministers. This word contains the revelation of the way of salvation through Jesus Christ. As the man who comes to God must believe that he is, and is the rewarder of them who diligently seek him, even under the dim light of the natural law, so the one who hears the clear and distinct voice of the Gospel must believe that "God was in Christ, reconciling the world unto himself, not imputing their trespasses unto them; and hath committed unto us [the apostles] the word of reconciliation." The next step which the believing hearer of the word from the mouth of an apostle had to take was to beg him to exercise his ministry of reconciliation toward himself. "We are ambassadors for Christ," says St. Paul, "as though God did beseech you by us: we pray you in Christ's stead, be ye reconciled to God."* The person who, recognizing the fact of a positive, or at least a negative, alienation of his soul from God, desired to close with this offer to make his peace with the Divine Majesty, must necessarily treat with his ambassador. He would ask from him the conditions of peace, the terms of reconciliation. The ambassador, having invited the enemies of his sovereign to a reconciliation, is in duty bound to make known to them in clear and precise terms what these conditions are. Without any doubt, the very first instructions given to their neophytes by the apostles contained a full explanation of the conditions they must comply with in order to obtain the grace of God and justification. A Protestant is bound to believe that these instructions have been distinctly and completely recorded in the New Testament—the only means, according to him, which God has provided for us, since the death of the inspired authors of that sacred collection, in order that we may know what these conditions are.

It is not necessary to spend time in proving that repentance from sin and conversion to God are conditions of salvation through Jesus Christ. The

---

* 2 Cor. v. 19, 20.

strictest Calvinist will admit this, and even maintain it strongly, notwithstanding his doctrine of justification by faith alone. In theory, he maintains that faith, as distinct from the love of God, is the sole instrument of justification; yet he does not hold that it can be true, justifying faith, separate from love. Practically, Calvinists generally make repentance and conversion, or a change of heart, the means and the test of the passage from the state of death to the state of life. Those who are not strict Calvinists, and who, with more or less explicitness, understand by saving faith *fides formata*, or faith informed by love, invariably make repentance and conversion the conditions of reconciliation with God, and the whole scope of their preaching is directed toward the end of awakening their hearers to a sense of their lost condition as sinners, and an earnest effort to obtain salvation from sin and its penalties by contrition for the past, and a sincere purpose of living a new life in the future. I may therefore take it for granted that the apostles taught those who believed their word, and who desired to act on that belief, that they must repent of their sins, resolve to sin no more, and begin to direct their intention and their actions toward their chief end, which is "to glorify God and enjoy him for ever." This resolution virtually includes obedience to all the commandments of God. He who wills the end wills the means. Whoever professes that he makes it the end of his life to glorify God here, in order that he may be glorified and beatified by him in eternity, must prove the reality of his purpose by keeping that law which God has laid down as the way by which this end must be attained. The only point which can be considered at all is, whether there are precepts in the law of Christ requiring something more than the mere internal acts of faith, hope, and charity as the condition of being made just and holy, a friend and child of God, and an heir of heaven. These internal acts undoubtedly comprise all the dispositions which are requisite to prepare the soul for the grace of God. But it is necessary that the soul should receive this grace, as well as be prepared and disposed for it. I am speaking now of a person who is still unregenerate, but who desires to receive the gift of regeneration, to obtain justification, to be reconciled with God, and admitted to the fellowship of his Son by adoption through his grace. Nothing which is done before regeneration can have any efficacy to efface sin or unite the soul with God. By faith the soul looks toward God as the author of grace and salvation. By hope it expects to receive from him this grace. By that charity which it is capable of exercising through the aid of prevenient grace before regeneration, and which is not filial, but only initial and servile love, or rather the fear of God, it turns its purpose and intention from the pleasures of sin to the eternal good. These are conditions precedent to regeneration and sanctification by the Holy Spirit. The actual communication of the sanctifying grace requires a distinct and positive act of God, by which he infuses into the soul his divine gifts, stamps his likeness upon it, and elevates it to a participation with his own nature. All this will be admitted by the disciples of the old Lutheran and Calvinistic confessions. I will therefore take it for granted for the present, and those who have abandoned or lost this old doctrine of their fathers may find it sufficiently proved from the Scripture in the course of what is to follow hereafter.

The question to be considered is, whether the apostles taught their catechumens to expect this illapse of the Holy Spirit to take place immediately in their souls after they had inwardly converted themselves to God, or taught them to resort to the sacraments as a medium and instrumental cause of sanctifying grace. This question is not difficult to answer in such a way as to satisfy completely any one who will calmly and attentively consider certain very clear texts of the New Testament, with his mind disposed to believe them in their plain, obvious sense, without regard to his preconceived opinions. St. Paul is particularly explicit and distinct in his teaching on this subject, and, when he speaks about the sacraments, his language is by no means "hard to be understood": although experience shows that it is easy to be passed over and neglected by those whose whole attention is absorbed by the most obscure, abstruse, and difficult portions of his writings.

The apostles, as I have already said, must have given their catechumens, at the very beginning of their Christian life, explicit and full instructions upon these topics, as being the very first principles of Christian doctrine. And St. Paul declares this expressly, at the same time distinctly mentioning some of these primary principles, in a passage which has been already cited in another connection. It is in the Epistle to the Hebrews, and forms one of those digressions into which the genius of his mind often led him, and which are often among the passages of his writings which are the most fraught with instruction and eloquence. "Ye have need," he says, "that one *teach you again* which be the *first principles* of the oracles of God." He calls them reprovingly mere Christian babes—that is, children or neophytes in the first class of the catechism. He reminds them that they learned their catechism a long time ago, when they were young in the faith and needed to be fed with the milk of the word. And he exhorts them to go forward, to ascend into a higher grade of Christian knowledge: "Therefore leaving the *principles of the doctrine of Christ,* let us go on unto perfection ; not laying again the foundation of repentance from dead works, and of faith toward God, of the *doctrine of baptisms,* and of *laying on of hands,* and of resurrection of the dead, and of eternal judgment."* The "doctrine of baptisms" is evidently the instruction concerning the nature of the sacrament of baptism, the way to receive it worthily, and the privileges and obligations involved in its reception. The use of the plural number appears strange and puzzling at first sight. But St. Paul was writing to converted Jews who were familiar with a similar rite in the Old Law, and knew of, if they had not received, the baptism of John. Wherefore the instruction concerning baptism necessarily included an exposition of the difference which distinguished the Christian sacrament from all other ceremonial ablutions, and this explains the reason for using the plural instead of the singular term, baptism. " Laying on of hands" can mean nothing else than the sacrament of confirmation. We see, then, most clearly, with what milk the apostles fed their Christian babes. The whole passage is unintelligible on the Calvinistic theory. It is irreconcilable with the Calvinistic doctrine. It teaches plainly the doctrine I have already estab-

* Heb. v. 12 ; vi. 1, 2.

lished concerning faith and the other prerequisites to justification. And it teaches, further, the primary importance of the sacraments, by classing the doctrine concerning baptism and confirmation among the "first principles," together with faith and repentance. This is incompatible with any kind of Protestant doctrine in which the grace of the sacraments, and their office as instrumental causes of sanctification, are denied. Mere ceremonies or outward rites, which signify, but do not confer, spiritual grace, are things of minor importance. And the context which follows evidently implies that the converts of the apostles had been taught by them to regard the sacraments of baptism, confirmation, and the Holy Eucharist as operative means of sanctification: "For it is impossible for those who were *once enlightened*, and have *tasted of the heavenly gift*, and were *made partakers of the Holy Ghost*, and have tasted the good word of God, and the powers of the world to come, if they shall fall away, to renew them again unto repentance." The term "enlightened," as every one who has read anything of primitive Christianity knows, is one of the specific terms appropriated to those who have received baptism. The "heavenly gift" is manifestly the Holy Eucharist; and the means of being made "partakers of the Holy Ghost" is shown to be the sacrament of confirmation by the connection of this passage with the one in which the laying on of hands is spoken of. Let it be observed that all these things are distinguished from the "word of God," and cannot therefore refer to faith or to mere internal acts excited by the preaching of the word. I repeat it: this whole passage is utterly irreconcilable with any Calvinistic or pretended evangelical theory which is based on Luther's doctrine of justification by faith alone, and excludes moral sanctity and sacramental grace from a share in justification. On the contrary, it is clear, harmonious, intelligible, and full of meaning and force so soon as it is read in the light of Catholic doctrine.

The Catholic catechumen who is under instruction from a priest in the principles of Catholic faith and practice is carefully taught the necessity and the mode of reforming his life and renouncing all sins and vicious habits. He is instructed in the articles of the faith as contained in the Creed and in the capital points of Christian doctrine. He is taught the nature and efficacy of the sacraments, especially baptism, confirmation, and the Holy Eucharist, and the way of preparing to receive them worthily. The future life is placed before his eyes as the end of his existence here, and he is admonished of the judgment which he must undergo when his probation is finished. When he has received the sacraments, he is admonished to aim at Christian perfection by the diligent use of the means of grace, the acquisition of virtue and holiness, and the practice of good works.

Precisely in the same manner does St. Paul describe the manner in which the apostles were accustomed to instruct their neophytes in the "principles of the doctrine of Christ." The first thing is "repentance from dead works"; turning away from the works of the dead—that is, deadly sins—and merely natural good works which are without life-giving power, to living works done in the grace of God. The next is "faith toward God," or the explicit knowledge and belief of the truths of divine theology. Then the doctrine of baptism and of the other sacraments. The young Christian is presented before us, after his instruction is completed, coming to the font of baptism to be "illuminated," sealed with the Holy Ghost by the laying on of the hands of an apostle, admitted to the Eucharistic Table of the Lord, and thus fully endowed with all the privileges of a child of God and an heir of heaven. Finally, he is exhorted to "go on unto perfection," not as one who is completely justified, saved, and secured by an extrinsic and imputed righteousness, but as one who has to work his own way in the favor of God and towards heaven, with the risk always attending him of forfeiting everything if he falls away and does not "show the same diligence to the full assurance of hope unto the end."

Among all the sacramental means and instruments of justification alluded to by the apostle, the first, the most necessary, and the one most closely connected with the primary and fundamental act which justifies a sinner, is the sacrament of baptism. We have already seen that the instruction given by the apostles to their neophytes respecting this sacrament was one of the first principles; and a part of the foundation of that Christian doctrine which they were required to believe, and according to which they were required to practise, as a preliminary to their reception into the number of the faithful. But we are not left to seek in casual allusions of this kind for the only light which the writings of the apostles themselves furnish us respecting the details of this instruction respecting baptism, or obliged to have our sole recourse to tradition, full and trustworthy as this source of knowledge is, for our more complete information on this topic. It so happens that there is scarcely any topic on which so many and such clear statements are found in the inspired writings of the apostles as this very one of baptism. This is a very happy circumstance for one who seeks after the truth respecting the Catholic faith in the New Testament, or who undertakes to prove it from the same. For the whole doctrine of the grace and sanctifying efficacy of sacraments, the entire principle of sacramental justification, is included and involved in that great and cardinal doctrine of the Catholic religion—the doctrine of baptismal regeneration. This doctrine established, and the way is clear and open to the demonstration of the whole Catholic system. This doctrine subverted, and every kind of anti-Catholic heresy has a clear field before it. It is therefore happy for us that the Scripture is so abundant and explicit in its teachings on this subject, as I shall now proceed to prove in the most satisfactory and unanswerable manner.

I begin by referring to one well-known and undeniable point of St. Paul's teaching throughout his Epistles, which is, that circumcision, together with other Jewish rites, was abolished because it was unprofitable as a means of justification—a mere sign and token of a covenant of grace, which became useless, and even noxious, when the covenant itself had been fulfilled. It is, therefore, absurd to suppose that a mere ceremony of baptism, really of no more value than circumcision, has been substituted in its place in the Christian Law. Protestants are wholly inconsequent when they attach so much importance to that which they regard as a mere ceremony, dispute so violently about the mode of performing it, and even make one particular mode of baptizing, and an opinion about the subjects who are fit to receive baptism, a sufficient reason for sectarian divisions among themselves. They will, of course, fall back on the precept of Jesus Christ, and declare that something which he has strictly commanded to be fulfilled cannot be a trivial matter. I admit it, and retort their argument on themselves. It cannot be a matter of trivial importance, for Jesus Christ would not make such a matter the object of a grave precept and obligation. But you make it a trivial matter by your explanation. Therefore your explanation is false. Let any one consider the solemnity of the form of baptism which is derived from the very words of our Lord himself: "I baptize thee in the name of the Father, and of the Son, and of the Holy Ghost." It is evident that such a form of words expresses a most momentous act, and denotes a relation established between the subject of baptism and the Blessed Trinity of the most sacred character. And that this is no other relation than that of "a child of God, a member of Christ, and an heir of the kingdom of heaven," involving the remission of all sin, original and actual, justification, sanctification, and every other grace or privilege which is included in regeneration or flows from it, I shall now proceed to prove by most explicit statements of the Holy Scripture.

I begin with the testimony of St. John Baptist:

"He that sent me to baptize with *water*, the same said unto me, Upon whom thou shalt see the Spirit descending, and remaining on him, the same is he which baptizeth with the *Holy Ghost*." * The baptism instituted by Jesus Christ was therefore not a mere outward lustration with water as a sign of something else, like that of John, but a real sacrament in which the Holy Ghost was given. This is reiterated and further explained by our Lord himself to Nicodemus: "Except a man be born of *water* and of *the Spirit*, he cannot enter into the kingdom of God." † The baptizing with the Holy Ghost is not, indeed, restricted to the sacrament of baptism, for it may be understood to include every kind of abundant outpouring of grace upon the minds and hearts of men. But it must have a special relation to that sacrament which is specifically called by the name of baptism. It is regeneration which is the term toward which all preparatory graces of the Holy Spirit tend, and from which all subsequent graces take their departure. Our Lord explained to Nicodemus the necessity of this regeneration and the sacramental medium by which it is effected, namely, the water of baptism. which is united as an outward sign with the inward and sanctifying grace of the Holy Spirit. There is an application of the general statement of St. John made

* St. John i. 33.   † St. John iii. 5.

by our Lord to the special instance of regeneration. The general statement is that it is characteristic of the ministry of Jesus Christ as the Son of God that he baptizes with the Holy Ghost. The particular statement of our Lord is that in the act of regeneration this baptism is one of water as well as of the Spirit. When, therefore, we find him instituting a sacrament which is specially called by that name which denotes the characteristic operation of his divine power, and in which the outward element is water, we must understand that this power is specially and signally manifested in this sacrament, and that its proper effect is to produce that new birth which he expressly declares to Nicodemus is caused by the union of "water and the Spirit." The outward ceremony of lustration with water and the name of baptism must have been chosen by our Lord for the primary and initiatory sacrament of his church, precisely because in this sacrament the baptism of the Spirit, which is the purification and sanctification of the soul by the grace proceeding from the Holy Spirit, is both represented and really imparted in a special manner.

As our Lord began his ministry by teaching the nature and necessity of baptism, not as a mere ceremony or sign which must be observed simply because he commanded it, like a Jewish rite, but as a true sacrament of regeneration, so he concluded it by a solemn repetition of the same doctrine. After his resurrection, "he appeared unto the eleven as they sat at meat, and upbraided them with their unbelief and hardness of heart, because they believed not them which had seen him after he was risen. And he said unto them, Go ye into all the world, and preach the gospel to every creature. He that *believeth and is baptized* shall be saved ; but he that believeth not shall be damned." * Here is a summary of the gospel, that is, the good tidings, or the announcement of the way of pardon and salvation to man. First, it is necessary to believe on Christ. Second, to receive his baptism. Everything is really included in these two conditions, although obscurely, and needing further elucidation in order that the idea which is formed in the mind of the way of salvation may become clear, distinct, and complete. This elucidation of faith has already been given, and we are now engaged in the elucidation of baptism. In a general way, it may be said that faith includes all the requisite dispositions which prepare the subject for baptism, and that baptism includes, together with the sacramental and sanctifying grace directly conferred by it, all the graces and privileges to which it gives a right, and all the obligations which it imposes.

The apostles fulfilled the commandment of their

* St. Mark xvi. 14-16.

Lord to the letter. Ten days after his ascension, the Vicar of Christ and Prince of the Apostles, St. Peter, preached the faith to a great assembly of Jews. As the conclusion and summary of his discourse, he exclaimed: "Therefore let all the house of Israel know assuredly, that God hath made that same Jesus, whom ye have crucified, both Lord and Christ." Behold the object of faith, on which it is necessary to believe as the first preliminary to pardon and salvation. "Now when they heard this, they were pricked in their heart, and said unto Peter and to the rest of the apostles, Men and brethren, what shall we do?" Behold here the beginning of faith, accompanied by a sincere disposition to act up to it, and that compunction of the heart which is the beginning of true repentance and conversion. "Then Peter said unto them, Repent, and *be baptized every one of you, for the remission of sins*, and ye shall receive the *gift of the Holy Ghost*." * Behold here the sacrament of baptism as the means of the remission of sins and sanctification by the grace of the Holy Spirit.

St. Paul, in his speech on the stairs of the castle at Jerusalem, cites the words spoken to him by Ananias at Damascus: "Arise, and *be baptized, and wash away thy sins*." † In the Epistle to the Romans he exclaims, appealing to a well-

---

* Acts ii. 36–38. † *Ibid.* xxii. 16.

known and familiar doctrine in which they had been instructed when they were made Christians: "Know ye not, that so many of us as were baptized into Jesus Christ were baptized into his death? Therefore we are *buried with him by baptism* into death." What is the meaning of being baptized into Jesus Christ? Evidently, being made a member of Christ by baptism. This is only another form of expressing that supernatural change called regeneration. The one who is a member of the fallen race of Adam, who is under the ban of original sin, and who is still further degraded and estranged from God by actual sins, is freed from the guilt of both original and actual sin, transferred from Adam to Christ, renewed and endowed with a new nature, born again of the Holy Spirit, through the merit of the death of Jesus Christ upon the cross. The old man of sin within him may therefore be said to have been crucified and buried in the death and burial of the Redeemer, who destroyed sin and death by dying for the expiation of the guilt and the remission of the penalty of sin. He is also raised to a new life after the model of Christ's resurrection. "Like as Christ was raised up from the dead by the glory of the Father, even so we also should walk in newness of life. For if we have been planted together in the likeness of his death, we shall be also in the likeness of his resurrection."* This "planting in the likeness of his death" is evidently the same thing as "buried with him by baptism into death." The destruction of sin and the creation of a new, supernatural life, whose consummation is everlasting beatitude, is therefore clearly and distinctly ascribed to baptism as the medium or instrumental cause by which the Holy Spirit operates in effecting the work of regeneration.

The apostle repeats the same thing to the Colossians, contrasting the operative power of the sacrament of baptism with the inefficacy of the rite of circumcision: "Ye are complete in him, which is the head of all principality and power; in whom also ye are circumcised with the circumcision made without hands, in putting off the body of the sins of the flesh by the circumcision of Christ: *buried with him in baptism, wherein also ye are risen* with him through the faith of the operation of God, who hath raised him from the dead." † In his First Epistle to the Corinthians he says that "by one Spirit are we all baptized into one body," ‡ and we must therefore understand him to refer to baptism in his Epistle to the Ephesians, in which he says: "Christ also loved the church, and gave himself for it; that he might sanctify and cleanse it *with the washing of water by the word"*; especially as he had already

* Rom. vi. 3–5.   † Col. ii. 10–12.   ‡ 1 Cor. xii. 13.

specified baptism as one of the great Unities: "Endeavoring to keep the Unity of the Spirit in the bond of peace: One Body, and One Spirit, even as ye are called in One Hope of your calling; One Lord, One Faith, *One Baptism*, One God and Father of all."* Finally, in the Epistle to Titus St. Paul evidently refers to baptism in the passage where he says that "after that the kindness and love of God our Saviour toward man appeared, not by works of righteousness which we have done, but according to his mercy he saved us, by the *washing of regeneration*, and renewing of the Holy Ghost." The Greek word λουτρον, translated by St. Jerome into the Latin *lavacrum*, signifies laver, or bath; and it is well known that the appellation "Laver of Regeneration," derived from this passage, is a common name for baptism among the Greek and Latin Fathers, as it is now among Catholics and Episcopalians. Even the editors of the American Bible Society's edition of King James's Version refer here to a passage in St. Peter's First Catholic Epistle, in which he distinctly mentions baptism, and which will be cited hereafter. The Protestant Bishop Bloomfield, annotating this passage, says: "Render, by 'the laver of regeneration.' The ancient expositors almost universally (see Chrys. i. 323), and all the most emi-

---

* Eph. v. 25, 26; iv. 3-6.

nent modern commentators, are agreed that by the παλιγγενεσία is meant *baptismal regeneration.*"* If the opinion of Bloomfield is held in light esteem as that of an Anglican, the judgment of Calvin ought to have some weight with his own disciples. Calvin renders the Greek phrase in the same manner with St. Jerome, by *lavacrum regenerationis*, and he goes on to say: "I doubt not that he at least alludes to baptism; indeed, I can easily allow the passage to be explained concerning baptism; not that salvation is included in the external symbol of water, but because baptism seals to us the salvation obtained by Christ. Paul is treating of the disclosure of the grace of God, which we have said is made manifest by faith. Since, therefore, a part of the revelation is made manifest by baptism—inasmuch, that is, as it is appointed for the confirmation of faith—he very suitably makes mention of it. Moreover, since baptism is the way of entrance into the church and a symbol of our grafting into Christ, it is here opportunely introduced by Paul, while he is endeavoring to show forth in what manner the grace of Christ has appeared to us; wherefore the construction of his argument is as follows: God has saved us by his mercy, of which salvation he has given the symbol and pledge in baptism, admitting us into his church and grafting

* Bloomf. Gr. Test. in loc.

us into the body of his Son. It is to be noted also that the apostles are accustomed to deduce an argument from the sacraments, that they may prove thereby the thing signified by them, for the reason that pious men ought to hold firmly this principle: that God does not *play with us by empty figures*, but *effects inwardly by his power that which he shows forth by the outward sign*. Wherefore baptism is fittingly and truly called the *laver of regeneration*. That man will rightly grasp the power and utility of the sacraments who so connects the thing and the sign that he does not make the sign something empty and inefficacious; nor, on the other hand, for the sake of exalting it, take away from the Holy Spirit what is properly his own. Yet, although the impious are neither washed nor renewed by baptism, it retains, notwithstanding, that power so far as relates to God, since, however much they may spurn the grace of God, it is nevertheless offered to them. Moreover, Paul is here addressing believers, in whom, because baptism is always efficacious, it is properly conjoined with its truth and effect." *

It is not my affair to vindicate the consistency of John Calvin—a matter which pertains to those who acknowledge him as their master. His way of playing fast and loose with doctrine, and his

* Calvin in Epist. Com. in loc.

shifty, sophistical habit of mind, are plainly enough exhibited in this passage. I have cited him simply for the purpose of showing that the language of Scripture and the deeply-seated sense of the Christian mind connect the sacrament of baptism so indissolubly with the grace of regeneration that only the deadening of that sense by a protracted action of heresy upon it can sever them. Let the reader take note of some of the admissions of Calvin in the passage above cited. He admits that baptism is the laver of regeneration. Now, the only plain and distinct sense which this phrase admits is that baptism is the sacrament in which the washing of regeneration is applied to the soul. He admits, moreover, that sacraments are not empty figures, but that the grace which they signify is effected by the power of God in all except the impious, in respect to whom baptism is denuded of sanctifying grace, not from any defect in itself, or lack of will on the part of God, but through their own fault, and because they spurn the grace offered to them. Once more, that baptism is always efficacious in true believers, and that all who are baptized would be washed and renewed by baptism if they were true believers. The objections which he covertly makes against the Catholic doctrine of baptism are that it makes the outward symbol of water to include salvation, and that it thereby detracts from the grace of the Holy Spirit. He seems also to insinuate that it teaches the sanctifying efficacy of baptism in the souls of the impious. Now, in point of fact, as Calvin knew very well, the Catholic Church ascribes no efficacy to the sacrament, except that of a secondary and instrumental cause, subordinated to the action of the Holy Spirit as the first cause and real author of regeneration; and, moreover, explicitly teaches that the unworthy recipient of baptism, who has not the requisite dispositions of faith and repentance, does not receive remission of sin and sanctifying grace when he is baptized, and cannot receive them until he has become a true penitent and a true believer. Therefore the Catholic doctrine respecting baptismal regeneration is fully justified by the admissions of Calvin. And I would beg of those Calvinists who admit that infants are proper subjects of baptism to note carefully what follows from the doctrine here laid down by their master, in regard to all baptized infants. It follows, namely, that they are regenerated. For, as the sign is efficacious by the institution of Jesus Christ in every case where the person who receives it does not defeat the gracious purpose of God by impiously spurning his grace, and as infants are incapable of any act of reason or will whatever, infants who are baptized cannot spurn the grace of God, and consequently are always washed and renewed in baptism, the laver of regeneration.

Quite similar to the passage from St. Paul's Epistle just explained is the one already alluded to in the First Catholic Epistle of St. Peter: "Once the long-suffering of God waited in the days of Noah, while the ark was a preparing, wherein few, that is, eight souls were saved by water. *The like figure whereunto even baptism doth also now save us* (not the putting away of the filth of the flesh, but the answer of a good conscience toward God), by the resurrection of Jesus Christ." *

Bishop Bloomfield expresses the sense of this passage as follows: "Into which a few (namely, eight) persons embarked, and were saved through the water, the antitype to which thing (namely, what corresponds to, and was figured by, the preservation of Noah and his family in the ark) doth now save us, through the resurrection of Christ, as the ark did *them:* [I mean] baptism, which is not merely the putting away the filth of the flesh [by material water], but the answer of a good conscience towards God." "By *doth now save us* is meant 'places us in a state of salvation.' *The answer of a good conscience toward God.* That is (as explains Mr. Holden), ' by that which ,enables us to return such an answer as springs from a good

---

* 1 Ep. St. Peter iii. 20, 21.

conscience towards God, which can be no other than the inward change and renovation wrought by the Spirit.' The meaning, therefore, is that baptism, in order to save us, must not be the mere outward act, but must be also accompanied with the inward grace ; in other words, it must be that baptism which our Lord described as the being born again of water and of *the Spirit.*" *

Calvin remarks upon this passage : " The sense is by no means ambiguous, that, Noe being saved by water, had a certain similitude of baptism. And the apostle calls this to mind, that the likeness between him and us may appear more clearly. I have already said that the scope of this passage is that we should not be led away by bad examples from the fear of the Lord and the right way of salvation, to mingle ourselves with the world. This appears clearly in baptism, in which we are buried together with Christ, that, being dead to the world and the flesh, we should live unto God. In this respect he calls our baptism an antitype to the baptism of Noe—not that the baptism of Noe was the original exemplar, while ours is an inferior figure, . . . since there is here no comparison of greater or less ; the apostle merely signifies that there is a mutual similitude, or, as it is commonly called, a correspondence, between the two. . . . There-

* Bloomf. in loc.

fore, as Noe obtained life by means of death, when he was shut up in the ark as if he had been in a tomb, and amid the general destruction of the world was preserved together with his little family, so, at the present time, the mortification which is represented by baptism is to us an entrance into life; nor is salvation to be hoped for unless we are separated from the world. *Not the putting away of the filth of the flesh.* . . . Some fanatical men (for instance, Schwenkfeld) vainly distort this testimony, desiring to take away all force and effect from the sacraments. For Peter did not here intend to teach that the institution of Christ is an empty and inefficacious thing, but only to exclude from the hope of salvation those hypocrites who, so far as lies in them, deprave and corrupt baptism. Moreover, when it is question of the sacraments, two things are to be considered—the sign and the thing, as in baptism the sign is water; but the thing is the ablution of the soul by the blood of Christ and the mortification of the flesh. The institution of Christ includes within itself each one of these. But that the sign often appears inefficacious and without fruit happens by the abuse of men, which does not take away the nature of the sacrament. . . . Certainly, when Peter, having made mention of baptism, immediately makes the exception that it is not the putting away of the filth of the flesh, he shows plainly enough that to some baptism is only of the latter, and therefore that the external sign is by itself of no value. *But the interrogation of a good conscience.* In the first place, *interrogation* is here employed in the place of answer or testimony. Moreover, Peter briefly defines the power and utility of baptism when he refers it to the conscience, and distinctly requires that confidence which can sustain the sight of God and stand before his tribunal. For in these words he teaches that baptism in its principal part is spiritual, and therefore that it includes in itself remission of sins and the reformation of the old man. For how can the conscience be good and pure, unless our old man has been converted, and we have been renewed to the righteousness of God? And how shall we answer before God, unless sustained and supported by the gratuitous pardon of sins?"*

I have quoted these passages from two Protestant commentators, in order to convince the Protestant reader that the texts referred to relate to baptism, and that the parenthesis in the text taken from St. Peter does not detract from their literal meaning and force. Bloomfield is admitted, by Calvinists even, to be a learned and accurate critic of the text of the New Testament. Calvin is their acknowledged master, and not only esteemed by

Calvin in loc.

them as a critical, but also as a doctrinal authority of the highest kind. Both concur in giving to the texts in question the same literal and exegetical interpretation with that which is given by the fathers and Catholic commentators. Baptism is the Laver of Regeneration, and the antitype of the salvation of the family of Noe by water. The spiritual renewal, of which the outward application of baptismal water to the body is the sacramental sign, is the inward and principal part of baptism. Peace of conscience and the reformation of the heart and life are the proper effects and consequences of this spiritual renovation. In the case of those persons to whom baptism is unprofitable, it is rendered unprofitable by their impiety and contempt of the grace of God. This is the sum of the doctrine extracted from the two texts cited, in the passages I have quoted from Calvin, and in which Bishop Bloomfield concurs. There are other sentences of Calvin in the context, which I have omitted because they are irrelevant to the precise point of reference, not being the elucidation of the literal meaning of the text, but discursions into the field of controversy. The Calvinistic tenet of justification by faith alone is, as I have said, wholly incompatible with the doctrine of sacramental justification. A Calvinist cannot consistently hold that baptism is anything more than a ceremony which signifies that regeneration which is effected by the immediate act of the Holy Spirit through the sole instrumentality of faith. All that Calvin can say, therefore, in respect to baptism, which sounds like orthodox doctrine, is either a gross contradiction to his own tenets or an illusory form of speech used in order to throw dust in the eyes of the simple. His followers have been more logical or more honest than himself, and have long ceased to think or speak of baptism as the laver of regeneration. It is of no consequence, however, in the interpretation of the Holy Scripture, to know what were the doctrinal tenets of Calvin, or what are those of his disciples. Although they are professedly derived from the Holy Scripture, they are derived by deduction, by reasoning, which is to a great extent very subtle and remote. The question before us is one which concerns a matter much more simple and obvious— namely, the examination of some very plain texts of Scripture, and of others which, if not so plain in themselves, become so by comparison with others and by the help of an analysis which is not very difficult. The only difficulty lies in prejudice. And on account of this prejudice I have taken more pains than would otherwise have been necessary, to show by Protestant authority that the texts I have cited refer to sacramental baptism.

These texts are now before the reader, and I ask him to consider their plain and obvious statements, and the sense which they convey to the mind when taken literally and combined with each other. They teach us that baptism is the laver of regeneration; that it has two parts—an outward lustration with water and an inward grace of the Spirit which produces a new birth; that by it we are saved, receive the remission of sins, are made members of the church and of Christ, are buried with Christ and raised up again with him, receive power to live a holy life, and are entitled to the resurrection of glory and life everlasting.

I will not refer to tradition and the doctrine of the primitive church as independent authorities. But it is reasonable even for a Calvinist to make use of both as a medium for getting a correct idea of the sense and meaning of the language used by the apostles. The constant and invariable interpretation of the fathers, and the unanimous teaching of the church during the first six centuries, are a proof of the understanding of the apostolic doctrine which was universal in the apostolic age, and must have been correct. Whoever desires to see the evidence of this unanimous teaching and belief of the Catholic doctrine of baptismal regeneration will find it in Dr. Pusey's learned tract on this subject, which was the eighty-second of the " Tracts for the Times."

Before proceeding any further, I may pause for a short time to answer some few objections and remove some difficulties which will doubtless perplex some of my readers, and hinder the assent which they should give to what has been thus far proved.

One may say that if the sacrament of baptism is the only appointed way of obtaining regeneration, there can be no salvation for those who are ignorant of the existence of the sacrament, or unable to receive it. This is very easily answered. The laws of God are binding on his subjects, but do not bind himself. He can work his own will without making use of the second causes and instruments which he chooses ordinarily to make use of. It is therefore just as easy for him to regenerate a soul without the sacrament of baptism as with it; and whenever fidelity to his promises or the merciful decrees of his providence make it fitting and good that he should do so, he undoubtedly does regenerate the soul by the immediate act of the Holy Spirit.

It may be said, again, that if the sacrament regenerates by its own intrinsic efficacy, a wicked man who receives baptism validly will be made a child of God and an heir of heaven without any inward and personal change from sin to holiness. This is not so. For, as has been already said, the want of a proper disposition in the subject prevents and suspends the due effect of the sacrament until his disposition is changed.

And once more, the sins committed by those who were certainly fit subjects for baptism, and therefore must have received its full effect when they were baptized, as in the case of all who were baptized in infancy, may be pointed at as an evidence that they never received sanctifying grace. But this objection springs altogether from the false conception of grace which belongs to the Calvinistic, but not to the Catholic, doctrine. According to Calvinism, grace works irresistibly, and can never be lost; wherefore one who is once regenerated can never fall back into a state of condemnation, but must go on, undergoing a progressive sanctification until he is finally glorified. I have already refuted this most false and pernicious opinion, and shall do so still more fully hereafter. At present I will merely state the true doctrine, in order to show how completely the objection disappears as soon as this doctrine is perceived. The grace of God works irresistibly only upon the subject who places no obstacle in the way of it by his own free-will. Every one who is in the exercise of his reason, therefore, can hinder the efficacy of grace if he will. Moreover, he must actively correspond to grace, and work with it, in order that it may produce in him the fruit of actual virtues and good works. Therefore, if he either resists and quenches grace in his soul by deadly sin, or neglects to coöperate with it by doing good works, he falls back into the state of spiritual death. The regenerate are placed on probation, as were Adam and Eve in their primitive state. They are free to keep the commandments of God or to break them. The majority do commit more or less sin, and some die impenitent. But this is no evidence that they were not regenerated in baptism. It proves that only infants are saved by baptism alone, and that therefore there are many other things necessary to an adult, that he may be saved, beside the grace of regeneration. But this is all it does prove.

The objection that the doctrine of sacramental regeneration interposes something between the soul and the Holy Spirit is futile. The blood of Christ is not the Holy Spirit, and yet no believer in the redemption of man by the death of our Lord will venture to deny that we are washed and sanctified by his blood. An instrument does not separate an effect from its cause, but brings it into contact with it. Christ is our Mediator by the operation of his human nature, as well as by that of his divine nature. And the intervention or interposition of his human nature with its proper operation between the human race and God does not divide, but unites, these two extremes. The

Holy Spirit acts as the efficient cause of the sanctification of men, proceeding from, and sent by the Son, equally with the Father; operating through the human nature and human operation of the same Divine Son as an instrumental cause. It is the Incarnation which interposes a medium between the human nature of men and the divine nature of the Holy Spirit—that is, of the Three Persons in God, the Father and the Son and the Holy Ghost, whose nature is one and the same. It is impossible, therefore, for a believer in the Incarnation to object to a sacramental instrument or medium, simply because it is something between the soul of man and the Divine Spirit.

Neither can he say that it substitutes another medium in place of the true medium between the human and divine nature, which is the humanity of Christ. It is not another, for it is subordinate to its principal, and the vehicle of its action. The virtue of the blood of Christ gives efficacy to the water of baptism. It is impossible to show that there is any necessary reason why the Mediator of Redemption should always exercise his office in his own proper person and by his own immediate acts. It is enough if he gives the authority and communicates the virtue which reside in him to subordinate agents and instruments, to transmit and communicate to individual men the effect of those essential acts which he has accomplished in his own person. His own institution and commandment prove that he has sanctified and consecrated visible elements and signs as the vehicle of his grace. And it is an insufferable piece of audacity, as well as a consummate folly, to raise an objection against the plain and obvious sense of his own words. It is our part to ascertain what are the sacraments, and what are their excellence and utility, from the evidence of the divine word, and to give our unhesitating, unwavering assent to that divine word, so soon as we apprehend it, without cavil or objection, without regard to our own prejudices or to the mere opinions of men. If there are difficulties existing in the mind without any wilful fault of the individual in whose mind they exist, it is right to seek for a solution. If they are solved in a satisfactory manner, so much the better. But if they are not completely removed, it is our strict duty to neglect them and pass them by, and to assent to revealed truth, in spite of all objections, as soon as it is sufficiently proposed. There are many antecedent difficulties which hinder a person brought up in the Calvinistic tenets from receiving the true doctrine of the sacraments, and other doctrines relating to the way of salvation which have a common principle in the Catholic doctrine of justification. I have briefly replied to some of these antecedent objections, and intend to do so still further in the course of this treatise. I cannot, however, do this at any great length, and must refer the reader who requires fuller explanations to other and more complete sources of instruction.

To return, therefore, to the principal thread of my discourse. I repeat again that I have given clear and sufficient proof from the Scripture of the doctrine of baptismal regeneration. That is to say, I have proved that baptism is a sacrament, instituted and endowed with an efficacious force by our Lord Jesus Christ, through which, as an instrument of his grace, the Holy Spirit imparts the gift of regeneration to every one who duly receives it. This has been proved in two ways—that is, by a negative and indirect argument, and by one which is direct and positive. It has been proved indirectly, by the refutation of the opposite and contrary doctrine of justification by faith alone. This doctrine starts from the assumption that God wills the salvation of the elect only; that for them alone Christ has died; and that by the simple fact of his meritorious death their salvation has been accomplished and secured. It explains the way by which they are redeemed as being a substitution of the Redeemer in their place, both to bear the punishment which is due to them, and to fulfil the obedience or righteousness which they owe to God, so that he is condemned for their sins imputed to him, and they are justified by his righteousness imputed to them. Faith is explained as a subjective apprehension and acceptance of this finished and complete justification and salvation, the instrument by which the elect are made to participate actually in the merits of Christ, which are theirs from eternity in the decree of God. This doctrine teaches, moreover, by logical necessity, that the justification which the elect hold by faith, being complete and absolute, can neither be diminished by sin nor increased by holiness, much less ever lost or forfeited after being once obtained. Sanctification is therefore a mere consequence and accidental quality of justification, which simply begins the preparation of the soul for the enjoyment of paradise, but is in no wise the formal cause of its acceptance before God or its final beatitude. The man who has faith is therefore always, though still personally a sinner, and continually committing sins which are worthy of death, in a state of perfect and unbroken friendship with God, and entitled to go immediately to heaven as soon as he dies. On this system, of course, sacraments are merely empty and useless forms to those who are not elected; and to those who are, simply signs of the grace they have already received or are destined to receive at a future time through faith.

In opposition to this doctrine, I have proved by an argument directly derived from the plain and obvious sense of the Holy Scripture, that God wills the salvation, and has provided in his Eternal and Incarnate Son for the salvation of the human race *en masse;* that, nevertheless, the salvation of individuals is not by this made secure and certain, but only possible, and is only actually secured by the fulfilment of certain further conditions, partly on the side of God, and partly on the side of man. On man's side, I have proved that faith is not the sole condition, but only the first among several, all alike essential. Moreover, that faith is distinctively a supernatural belief in the truths of divine revelation, and, together with repentance and a resolution to keep God's commandments, constitutes the necessary and proper disposition in an adult person for receiving regeneration and sanctifying grace. I have also proved that the internal justifying principle, or formal reason whereby one is really made and accounted just before God, is *fides formata*, or the habit of faith informed and vivified by charity or the love of God. This *fides formata*, which is the living, active principle of a new nature, and is communicated by the Holy Spirit, can only be given by the regeneration of the soul, which is dead by original sin, and by actual sin also if the guilt of actual sin has been incurred. The only question is, therefore, How is the grace of regeneration imparted? There is no reason why it should not be given through baptism; for there are none of the conditions which precede baptism, which either singly or conjointly demand for their verification that the subject in whom they exist should be already justified. The negative and indirect proof of baptismal regeneration is therefore perfect.

The positive proof is contained in the repeated and distinct declarations of our Lord and the apostles, which I need not now resume. It is most clear and certain that a person desiring to be saved, and coming to one of the apostles to learn the way of salvation, would be taught that God had provided for him in Jesus Christ all that was requisite, and that he could therefore secure his own salvation by fulfilling certain conditions: that he must believe in Jesus Christ and his doctrine, must detest and renounce sin, resolve to begin a new life and keep the commandments, and, after suitable preparation, come to the font of baptism, where he would receive regeneration, remission of sins, and a complete justification through the merits of Christ.

The exposition of the true Catholic doctrine of the Way of Salvation as contained in the Holy Scripture is now, therefore, up to a certain point, complete. " Baptism doth also now *save us* by the resurrection of Jesus Christ," as the Prince of the Apostles declares in plain terms. A Calvinist might easily conclude from this that the matter is now ended, and that one who has been made by baptism a child of God, a member of Christ, and an heir of the kingdom of heaven, has acquired an indefeasible and inamissible right to eternal salvation. He is accustomed to consider the matter as settled once for all between the soul and God as soon as the individual has received justification and regeneration; that he has been transferred irrevocably from death to life, and can never more incur eternal condemnation. But this is a great mistake. The very idea of justification by a real sanctification which is inherent in the subject, in opposition to that which is by an imputation of a righteousness extrinsic to the subject, makes the continuance and perpetuity and consummation of this justice dependent on the permanence of the personal sanctity of the subject of grace. Only the infant, or the adult who departs from this life immediately after baptism, receives a finished salvation by baptism alone. The one who attains to the use of reason, and is subjected to a probation and trial, must keep his sanctity by making those holy acts in which the principle of supernatural life becomes operative. How can faith which worketh by love subsist, except by acts of faith and love? If the inward principle of justification is destroyed by sins against faith or charity, the justification which depends on it must be lost. Unless, therefore, every baptized person receives a grace which efficaciously and infallibly prevents him from sinning, he may sin and lose the grace of God; and unless he receives an infallible gift of perseverance, he may be finally lost. No one will pretend that baptism gives a right either to confirmation in grace or to final perseverance. It is the beginning of salvation, it places the soul in the state of grace and salvation, but it is necessary that many other graces should be given, and many conditions fulfilled, in order that the inheritance of the kingdom of heaven may be actually obtained in possession.

We may conclude, therefore, that there ought to be more sacraments than one. We find that it is the pleasure of the divine Mediator and King of men to grant regeneration and remission of sins through a sacrament. We learn from this example what is the nature of a sacrament. And we therefore conclude that the Lord, who always acts by fixed laws and according to a plan, has provided all the other sacraments which are requisite to complete the work begun in baptism, and that they are all of the same essential nature, considered as to their generic or sacramental entity. We conclude also the institution of a New Law in place of the Old

Law, in which there is the most clear and ample code of doctrinal, religious, and moral precepts, directing the Christian what he must believe and what he must do in order to attain his end, everlasting salvation. It is evident, therefore, that my work is not yet finished in showing how one is to obtain the beginning of salvation, and pointing out the gate of entrance into the way of life. It is necessary to point out, still further, what are the most essential means and conditions to be used and complied with, in order that one may walk in that way to the end, and pass out of the opposite gate which opens into life eternal.

CHAPTER FOURTH.

Necessity of Means for tne Remission of Sin after Baptism—Venial and Mortal Sin—The Sacrament of Penance—Extreme Unction—Purgatory—Means for the Preservation and Increase of Grace and Holiness—The Holy Eucharist the great Source of Grace and Nourishment for the Soul.

WHOEVER believes in regeneration, or the new birth of the Holy Spirit, must admit that it produces in the renewed and forgiven sinner, together with the abolition of original and actual sin, a new and holy principle of spiritual life and activity. He is born of God, after the image of Jesus Christ, and bears therefore in himself the likeness of the Eternal Son, who is the image of the Father; and is also the temple of the Holy Spirit, who dwells in him with his sevenfold gifts. The image of Christ cannot coexist with the image of Satan in the soul, or the Holy Spirit dwell in a soul which is under the dominion of sin. The principle of life excludes the principle of death, and *vice versâ ;* and therefore sanctifying grace excludes all deadly sin, and deadly sin extinguishes sanctifying grace. The soul which has been made alive must continue to live and exercise the functions and acts of spiritual life; otherwise it lapses into the state of death, from which it can only be recovered by a new spiritual resurrection. I have already proved that a mere trust in the merits of Christ, which the Calvinists call faith, cannot of itself give life to the soul or make it just before God, and that faith, taken in its true sense, is a dead faith, and therefore not life-giving, unless it is joined with charity. It is, therefore, the living faith working by love, or *fides formata*, which is the principle of spiritual life, and must be preserved if one would continue in grace, and must persevere until death if one would hold out to the end in the friendship of God and never forfeit the rights of his baptism. It belongs to the very essence of the love of God that this love be supreme and exclude all contrary love of self and other creatures. That is, it is necessary that God should be the final end toward which the intention is directed, and that no creature should be substituted for God as the final end or chief good. He who wills the end wills the means; and therefore he who directs the intention of his will to God must keep the laws he has made in order to direct all moral actions toward their final end. Sin consists in turning from God to the created good as our final end, by a voluntary transgression of one of these precepts. Whoever sins, by the very fact turns himself from God as his final end, and thereby violates the principle of charity, acts on a directly opposite and contrary principle. This contrary principle has therefore expelled the principle of charity from his soul, and extinguished its spiritual life. Keeping the commandments of God and avoiding all grievous sins is, then, a necessary condition which the regenerate man must fulfil in order to remain in the state of justification. It follows from this that God gives to the baptized sufficient grace to keep his law, and that by the aid of grace it is possible to go from the baptismal font to the grave without ever staining the robe of innocence by a single grievous sin. It is too plain to need proof that it is also easy to sin. And if one sins, the same grace which at first sanctified him must sanctify him again, or he is lost for ever. The goodness and mercy of God, who wills the salvation of all men so long as their probation continues, must have provided special means for increasing and strengthening spiritual life in the living, and for raising again and purifying the fallen and guilty. The Way of Salvation is therefore a way provided by our Lord Jesus Christ, in which Christians work out their salvation and advance toward heaven by keeping the commandments, with special means for obtaining strength and perseverance, and other means for obtaining pardon and purification when they fall by the way and defile themselves by sin.

All this, which is only a just and necessary deduction from the truths already proved from the Holy Scripture, is capable of its own separate and independent proof from the same divine source. And this proof I shall now proceed to give.

The language of St. Paul is perfectly plain and explicit on this subject: " There is therefore now no condemnation to them which are in Christ Jesus." All sins have been remitted, and they have no guilt upon them which requires an eternal punishment. But who are they who are in Christ Jesus? They are those "who walk not after the flesh, but after the Spirit." How have they been freed from condemnation and enabled to walk after the Spirit, that is, by the inspiration and aid of grace to live a life holy and free from sin? " There is *therefore* now no condemnation. . . . *For* the law of the Spirit of life in Christ Jesus hath made me *free from the law of sin and death.*" Christ, having by his death expiated sin and merited grace, has conferred on the regenerate a power which is above the forces of nature, to keep that law which they otherwise would be morally unable to keep so entirely and perfectly as to be free from all sin. " For what the law could not do, in that it was *weak through the flesh,* God sending his own Son in the likeness of sinful flesh, and for sin, condemned sin in the flesh: that the righteousness *of the law* might be *fulfilled in us, who walk not after the flesh, but after the*

Spirit." Walking after the Spirit means, therefore, fulfilling the righteousness of the law or keeping the commandments of God. This is confirmed by what follows in the context: "The carnal mind is enmity against God: for it is not subject to the law of God, neither indeed can be." The argument of this passage is easily converted into a regular syllogism.

All that which is not subject to the law of God is enmity against God. But the carnal mind is not subject to the law of God. Therefore the carnal mind is enmity against God. The apostle proceeds then to draw the necessary inference that whoever has a carnal mind has enmity against God, or is the enemy of God, and consequently is the object of God's enmity. "So then they that are in the flesh cannot please God." Walking after the flesh, therefore, means not being subject to—that is, violating—the law of God, or sinning. Whoever sins must then become the enemy of God and incur the penalty of death. "To be carnally minded is death." "If ye live after the flesh, ye shall die." In other words, mortal sin is the death of the soul. And consequently, whoever is in the state of sanctifying grace and of friendship with God must be free from mortal sin, must fulfil the righteousness of the law, must keep all the commandments of God, and preserve his justification by preserving the inward sanctity given him in baptism and persevering in good works. This is expressly declared by St. Paul in a distinct statement: "But ye are not in the flesh, but in the Spirit, if so be that the Spirit of God dwell in you." "If ye through the Spirit do mortify the deeds of the body, ye shall live. For as many as are led by the Spirit of God, they are the sons of God."*

St. John teaches the same doctrine: "Beloved, now are we the sons of God. . . . Whosoever committeth sin transgresseth also the law: for sin is the transgression of the law. . . . He that committeth sin is of the devil. . . . Whosoever is born of God doth not commit sin; for his seed remaineth in him: and he cannot sin, because he is born of God. In this the children of God are manifest, and the children of the devil: whosoever doeth not righteousness is not of God."† It is plain, then, that a person who is the child of God and led by the Spirit cannot commit deadly sin while he is a child of God, or that the state of filial love and the state of sin cannot exist at the same time in the same person. St. John expressly teaches that the principle of sanctifying grace excludes sin by its very nature, and that the principle of sin excludes sanctifying grace, which is the spiritual life of the soul, and consequently produces

---

* Rom. viii. 1–16.   † 1 Epistle St. John iii. 2–10.

death, or rather, is itself the death of the soul, by its very nature.

The justified man can therefore fall from the state of justification, and he does so fall whenever he commits a grievous and deadly sin. Moreover, he can die in that state, and incur eternal condemnation. It is evident from what has been already proved that if he sins he falls from grace, and consequently, if he dies without forgiveness, must be lost for ever. It is also manifest that he can sin, unless he is confirmed in grace; and persevere in sin to the end, unless he has received an indefeasible gift of final perseverance. But the gift of regeneration does not include in itself either of these gifts, which are additional and purely gratuitous gifts, even in the case of the adopted and justified sons of God, however holy they may be.

God, through the prophet Ezekiel, declared to the people of Israel that they were to live by keeping his commandments, and should die if they broke them. "I am the Lord your God; walk in my statutes, and keep my judgments, and do them, . . . which if a man do, he shall even live in them." "But when the righteous turneth away from his righteousness, and committeth iniquity, and doeth according to all the abominations that the wicked man doeth, shall he live? All his righteousness that he hath done shall not be mentioned; in his trespass that he hath trespassed, and in his sin that he hath sinned, in them shall he die." * So also St. Peter: " If after they have escaped the pollutions of the world through the knowledge of the Lord and Saviour Jesus Christ, they are again entangled therein, and overcome, the latter end is worse with them than the beginning. For it had been better for them not to have known the way of righteousness, than, after they have known it, to turn from the holy commandment delivered unto them. But it is happened unto them according to the true proverb, The dog is turned to his own vomit again; and the sow that was washed to her wallowing in the mire." † And St. Paul: " If we sin wilfully after that we have received the knowledge of the truth, there remaineth no more sacrifice for sins, but a certain fearful looking-for of judgment and fiery indignation." " Leaving the principles of the doctrine of Christ, let us go on unto perfection. . . . And this will we do, if God permit. For it is impossible for those who were once enlightened, and have tasted of the heavenly gift, and were made partakers of the Holy Ghost, and have tasted the good word of God, and the powers of the world to come, if they shall fall away, to renew them again unto repentance; seeing they crucify to themselves

* Ezek. xx. 19, 21; xviii. 24. † 2 Epistle St. Peter ii. 20–22.

the Son of God afresh, and put him to an open shame." *

It would be easy to multiply proofs from all parts of the Holy Scripture of the doctrine that man is accounted before God as just or righteous on the ground of a real, personal, and inherent righteousness, whose principle is a grace of sanctification imparted by the Divine Spirit, while its operation consists in doing good works; and which may be, as it too often is, destroyed by the commission of sin. Those which have been given are, however, amply sufficient. Such being the case, it becomes a most momentous question what provision our Lord has made for the forgiveness of sins after baptism, and the restoration of the grace which has been lost.

A truly earnest and sincere person who really desires to give his whole attention to the work of securing the permanent and eternal union of his soul with our Lord Jesus Christ, and whose mind is imbued with Calvinistic and puritanical ideas, will very naturally find much to trouble and perplex him in the passages just cited from the Holy Scripture, and others of a like tenor. On the one side, he cannot fail to see that he must be saved from the dominion of sin, and keep the commandments of God in all points, if he would obtain peace of conscience and a reasonable assurance of the friendship

* Heb. x. 26, 27.

of God. On the other, his extremely rigorous views of the divine law and of the guilt and penalty attached to the smallest offences, as well as to the involuntary and unavoidable movements of what he calls inbred or indwelling sin, must make it appear to him to be morally or even physically impossible to obtain and practise that holiness which seems to him sufficiently perfect to satisfy the inexorable demands of the divine justice. And if he examines the New Testament to find out how far and by what means he can obtain a sure pardon for the sins he has committed since the time of his baptism, he will be still more bewildered by the paucity and obscurity of the statements which it contains, and by the apparent teaching of some passages that there are sins which are unpardonable. Every one who is familiar with the religious biography of the Calvinistic sects knows how deeply tinged with melancholy is that which is called the religious experience of those who have been the most noted for piety among them. The fearful spectre of the " unpardonable sin " has haunted the imagination of many a one among them, and those who have read Bunyan's " Pilgrim's Progress " cannot have forgotten the striking and fearful picture there given of the man at the Interpreter's house, who had " sinned away his day of grace." From the same cause, those members of the Church of England who began the great movement of Oxford, while they revived the old Catholic doctrine of baptismal regeneration and justification by inherent righteousness, set forth in the darkest colors the enormity of post-baptismal sin, and the uncertainty as well as difficulty of obtaining remission of its guilt. The mixture of certain Catholic with certain other Calvinistic elements makes a most fearful compound. Jansenists and a certain class of Anglicans have accordingly made out of the easy yoke and light burden of the religion of Christ something as torturing and unbearable as the cangue which the tyrants of Tonquin lay on the necks of their prisoners. And it is therefore with the greatest justice and reason that Bishop McIlvaine has denounced the insupportable rigor of a system which combines that which is most severe in both the Catholic and the Protestant doctrines, without presenting to the penitent sinner the provision of mercy contained in either. With the utmost logical force the same writer shows that the fundamental Catholic principle of justification must either be rejected totally or followed up to all its consequences by embracing the whole Catholic doctrine of the Way of Salvation.* A law which is above the condition of human nature, even in its regenerate state, is the despair of all men; and one which does not contain ample provision for mercy

* *Vid.* McIlvaine on Oxford Divinity.

and pardon is the despair of all sinners. It is necessary, therefore, to examine, in the first place, what that law is, and what are the sins which bring its eternal penalty upon the conscience; and afterwards to consider the means of pardon which have been provided.

That human nature remains in some respects in the state to which it was degraded by the sin of Adam, after it has been regenerated in Christ, no one can possibly question who believes in the doctrine that Adam was endowed with the gifts of integrity and immortality, and lost them by the fall. It is just as certain that concupiscence remains in the regenerate as that the doom of death still remains upon them. St. Paul calls this remaining effect of original sin a "law of sin." "I delight in the law of God after the inward man: but I see another law in my members, warring against the law of my mind, and bringing me into captivity to the law of sin which is in my members."* It is not necessary to discuss the question how far this and other texts connected with it refer to the unregenerate or the regenerate state. That the sinner is in captivity to, or under the servitude of this law, before he is liberated by grace, is evident. The justified man may be said to be also in captivity in a different sense. That is, he is under the

* Romans vii. 22, 23.

painful bondage which ties his immortal spirit to a frail, mortal body which weighs it down, and makes it necessary to struggle against infirmities and temptations. But that he is freed from the captivity of sin, or from the dominion of this law in the members by the grace of Christ, is expressly declared by St. Paul: "For when we were in the flesh, the motions (rendered in the margin *passions*) of sins, which were by the law, did work in our members to bring forth fruit unto death. But now we are delivered from the law, that being dead wherein we were held."* And again: "If Christ be in you, the body is dead because of sin; but the Spirit is life because of righteousness. . . . Therefore, brethren, we are debtors, not to the flesh, to live after the flesh. For if ye live after the flesh, ye shall die: but if ye through the Spirit do mortify the deeds of the body, ye shall live." † Evidently, St. Paul teaches that there is a conflict in the regenerate between the superior nature co-operating with grace and the inferior nature with its concupiscence, in which the just man is victorious. He is not free from the inclination and temptation to sin, nor can he expel from himself or forcibly quell the repugnance and resistance of his lower nature to the dictates of reason and the Holy Spirit. But he can, and while he remains just he does, with his deliber-

---

* Romans vii. 5, 6. † *Ibid.* viii. 10, 12, 13.

ate free-will obey the law of God and refrain from grievous and deadly sins, as I have already proved. Concupiscence and its involuntary motions are not, therefore, called sin in the proper sense of the word. They can only be called sin improperly, because they come from sin and lead to sin; and therefore they can and do co-exist with the state of grace and with true Christian righteousness. Sin, in the active sense, is voluntary transgression of God's law, and in the passive sense the death of the soul, produced by transgression. The just man is therefore free from sin. " For the law of the Spirit of life in Christ Jesus hath made me free from the law of sin and death." * "Whosoever abideth in him sinneth not." † Yet the inclination to sin and the involuntary, indeliberate first motions of the law of sin and death in the lower nature remain in the just. Wherefore they are not sin, and do not separate the soul from God.

Nevertheless, St. James declares that "in many things we offend all," ‡ and St. John, that "if we say we have no sin, we deceive ourselves." § None but deluded victims of spiritual pride will pretend that it is morally possible to avoid all sins for any considerable length of time without an extraordinary grace. We are obliged to confess ourselves to

---

* Romans viii. 2.   ‡ St. James iii. 2.
† 1 Epistle St. John iii. 6.   § 1 Epistle St. John i. 8.

be sinners, or else to be manifest hypocrites, so great is the fragility and inconstancy of human nature, even in the most perfect. If every sin, therefore, however minute and inconsiderate it may be, destroy the life of the soul and merit eternal death, the Gospel of Christ is of very little value to us, and our prospects are very gloomy for salvation. How, then, can we say, "There is therefore now no condemnation to them which are in Christ Jesus,"* or that "his commandments are not grievous"? † There is no way out of this difficulty without making the distinction of the Catholic doctrine between mortal and venial sin. It is necessary to admit that there are sins which destroy the life of grace, and sins which do not destroy this life, but only injure more or less the health and strength and beauty of the soul.

When we consider the question how sins are to be remitted and the soul delivered from their guilt and stain, the difficulty of deciding this most important matter from the Scripture alone becomes very great. In regard to venial sins there is no special difficulty. For the love of God in a soul united to him by grace is evidently sufficient to expel venial sin, if one will only make an effort to increase this love, and resolve to obey its impulse in all things, small as well as great. This applies to

---

* Romans viii. 1 † 1 Epistle St. John v. 3.

the habit of venial sin, or tepidity in the service of God. And as to sins of inconsideration, they are easily effaced as fast as they are committed, by those acts which are made so soon as a person recollects himself and reflects on the actions of the day. Moreover, there are numerous passages in the Holy Scripture, familiar to all who read it, which express the willingness of God to forgive these faults and trespasses of his children as soon as they sincerely ask pardon.

But in regard to mortal sin, any one who seeks to find out from the New Testament alone, by his own study, how one who has again incurred death and condemnation after receiving baptism is to be restored, will find himself very much perplexed. What sins are mortal, whether any or every mortal sin is remissible, and, if so, by what means, are most momentous and practical questions, on which it is necessary to have clear and explicit information. This will be looked for in vain, and certain passages which I have already cited appear to teach that there are irremissible sins, without clearly specifying which they are. To these I add now one more: "All manner of sin and blasphemy shall be forgiven unto men: but the blasphemy against the Holy Ghost shall not be forgiven unto men. And whosoever speaketh a word against the Son of man, it shall be forgiven him: but whosoever speaketh against the Holy Ghost, it shall not be forgiven him, neither in this world, neither in the world to come."* And St. Paul says of one who sins wilfully after receiving the knowledge of the truth, that he "*hath done despite unto the Spirit of grace.*"†

St. John appears to say that there is no use in praying for one who has committed mortal sin. "If any man see his brother sin a sin which is not unto death, he shall ask, and he shall give him life for them that sin not unto death. *There is a sin unto death: I do not say that he shall pray for it.*"‡ Yet the expression, "give him life for them that sin not unto death," indicates that mortal sin is referred to in the former as well as the latter clause, since one who has need to be restored to life is dead. And St. James says that "he which converteth a sinner from the error of his way shall *save a soul from death.*"§ St. Paul, also, sanctioned the absolution of a sinner at Corinth whom he had excommunicated for taking his step-mother to wife—certainly a grievous sin. That those who sin grievously after baptism are not altogether shut out from the hope of pardon may be regarded as taught with sufficient explicitness in the Scripture. But what is needed is the assurance that there is remission for

* St. Matthew xii. 31, 32.
† Hebrews x. 29.
‡ 1 Epistle St. John v. 16
§ St. James v. 20.

every sinner and for all sins, and definite information about the conditions of pardon. This will be sought for in vain so long as we confine ourselves exclusively to the texts of Scripture. A Catholic has the authority of tradition and of the church to interpret the Scripture and supply what is lacking in it. But the Scripture itself furnishes only one perfectly clear and explicit statement on the subject, which is that sins are remitted by the power of the keys which Christ committed to the apostles: " Receive ye the Holy Ghost : whosesoever sins ye remit, they are remitted unto them."* This is very clear so far as it goes. It proves that the apostles could remit sins. And we may deduce from it with great probability that, since the power is conceded without any express limitation, it was unlimited, and that, in order to be exercised judicially, it implies confession of sins on the part of the penitent. Yet if the difficulty should occur to the mind of one seeking after the truth, that these very apostles have declared some sins to be irremissible, what solution could he find which is perfectly satisfactory ? Our Lord said also : " Whosesoever sins ye shall retain, they are retained." And what if, in the passages cited above, they have declared that some sins are always retained and never remitted ? A supreme court defines its own powers, and its judgments are

* St. John xx. 22, 23.

the authentic interpretation of the law. It is necessary, therefore, to have recourse to this apostolic tribunal, to this authority which bears the keys of the kingdom of heaven, in order to ascertain what sinners can be absolved, what sins can be remitted, and what are the conditions to be complied with by the penitent.

The Scripture conducts us, as it were, to the very door of the Sacrament of Penance, but no further. It is impossible to understand clearly and with perfect certitude what it really does teach respecting the remission of sins after baptism, without recurring to the Unwritten Word, the doctrine which Christ taught the apostles, but which they did not record, leaving it to the channel of oral tradition and the teaching of their successors, to whom they bequeathed their power. When the light of this Catholic doctrine is turned on the inspired written documents of faith, we are enabled to see clearly that sense which was before obscure, and to read in them sufficient indications of the way of salvation from sin committed after baptism, whether venial or mortal, and from its temporal or eternal penalties.

This Catholic doctrine teaches that there is no sin which is unpardonable, and that every sinner, however numerous or grievous his sins, may be forgiven and saved, if he will repent. The declarations with which the Holy Scripture abounds of the mercy of God are therefore to be understood in their universal and unlimited sense, in reference as well to those who have been baptized as to those who have not. Those obscure and difficult passages which seem to make exceptions in respect to the remission of sins by the power of the keys, must therefore be interpreted in harmony with this doctrine. The most alarming and perplexing of all these texts—one which St. Augustine says is not exceeded in difficulty by any passage of the whole Scripture—places, indeed, as much apparent limitation on the efficacy of baptism as on that of absolution by the power of the keys. I refer to the text from St. Matthew respecting the sin against the Holy Spirit, which sin, whatever it may be, can be committed by a person who has not been baptized as well as by a recreant Christian. In fact, the very occasion of this terrible sentence from the lips of the Judge of men was a blasphemy of certain Pharisees who had never received the baptism of Christ. If baptism has the power of washing away all sin, therefore, notwithstanding what our Lord said of the sin against the Holy Spirit, there is no reason why absolution may not remit this same sin, and, *à fortiori*, all lesser sins, if the sinner is a baptized person. And as it is a settled point of Catholic doctrine that baptism and absolution can remit all sins without any exception, the passages of Scripture which appear to affirm the contrary must be interpreted in harmony with this doctrine, and with the far more numerous declarations of the Scripture by which this doctrine is supported. The church gives us only a negative exposition; that is, excludes every interpretation which restricts the efficacy of baptism and absolution. For the positive exposition she refers us to the fathers and other learned commentators. From these we may gather as a general result sufficient for our purpose, that the sin against the Holy Spirit is some kind of peculiarly wilful and obstinate resistance and opposition to the supernatural light and grace of the Spirit of God. It is called irremissible, either because it is devoid of any of those palliations which are found in ordinary sins of human fragility, and which, in a certain sense, appeal to the compassion of God, or because there is scarcely any hope that one who commits it will ever repent of it. And so in respect to the other passages cited. They are satisfactorily explained if, on the one hand, we understand them as alluding to the well-known fact that no second regeneration, no repetition of baptism, is possible, and that no other sacrament is equal to baptism as a sacrament of the dead; and, on the other, as renewing the same statement which our Lord made concerning the sin against the Holy Ghost. Those whose sins proceed from a deliberate and contumacious spirit of contempt of the grace of God are with difficulty and but rarely brought to repentance, and they commonly die in that final impenitence which is the natural consequence of their total apostasy from God. Nevertheless, they can, and sometimes, by an extraordinary grace, they do, repent; and if they do, they can be absolved from their sins, whatever their number and enormity, and even at the last moment of life.

This difficulty being disposed of, we return again to our point of departure, which is that ample means have been provided for the remission of sins after baptism. Since it has pleased God to regenerate the fallen child of Adam by a sacrament, the analogy of reason and faith requires that there should be another sacrament for his restoration, in case he should fall from grace, as he is continually liable to do through temptation and human fragility. The existence, nature, and conditions of this sacrament are not distinctly and explicitly taught in the inspired, apostolic writings, like those of baptism. But when one already knows the institution and nature of the sacrament of penance, certain things about it are seen to be clearly contained in the Scripture, and other things to be obscurely involved in its statements, from which they can be deduced by just and logical inference.

I am not about to prove the divine institution of the sacrament of penance. I simply assert, as an historical fact, that the Catholic Church from the times of the apostles has testified to the unbroken succession of priests from our Lord, who have received from him power to absolve from all mortal sins committed after baptism those who are penitent and who confess their sins. Those who desire to have the evidence of this historical fact are referred to the books which contain it. Taking for granted this fact, the sense of the famous passages regarding the absolving power in the New Testament becomes obvious. The power of the priest to absolve is seen to be clearly taught in them, and the obligation of the penitent to confess is inferred from the very nature of the act.

When the sacrament of extreme unction is known to have been also administered in the Catholic Church from the apostolic age, the sense of an otherwise obscure passage in the Epistle of St. James becomes perfectly clear, and furnishes a fair Scriptural proof of both sacraments. "Is any sick among you? let him call for the elders of the church; and let them pray over him, anointing him with oil in the name of the Lord: and the prayer of faith shall save the sick, and the Lord shall raise him up; and if he have committed sins, they shall be forgiven him. Confess your faults one to another, and pray one for another, that ye may be healed." * Elder, in this passage, is the same as presbyter, and priest is only the ancient English contracted form of presbyter. Therefore the Douay translation, " let him bring in the *priests of the church,*" besides being much more explicit and in accordance with the language in use before the schism of the sixteenth century among all Christians, than that of King James, is equally literal. Forgiveness of sins is ascribed to this sacrament in the text. And the doctrine of the Catholic Church makes the sense plain in this respect also. Venial sins are remitted directly, the effects of mortal sin are removed, and indirectly even mortal sins are remitted, by the sacrament of extreme unction. Confession is spoken of in such a way that if we suppose Christians in the apostolic age to agree in doctrine with the present Catholic Church, they must have understood it as referring to the confession of the sick man to the priest who came to anoint him. King James's Version has "faults" where the Douay has "sins," as the translation of the Greek παραπτωματα, Vulgate *peccata.* This translation, though verbally correct, veils the

* St. James v. 14-16.

meaning, and induces the reader to think that the passage refers to a mere acknowledgment of little defects which may be made by friends in confidential conversation. The Greek word is the same used by St. Paul (Rom. v. 25) to denote the offences for which Christ died. Those who can read Latin will perceive in St. Jerome's version a much clearer and more precise rendering of the original text than our clumsy language can give, and will see how evident the true sense must have been to his mind, imbued with ancient and apostolic traditions: "Infirmatur quis in vobis? inducat presbyteros ecclesiæ, et orent super eum, ungentes eum oleo in nomine Domini; et oratio fidei salvabit infirmum, et alleviabit eum Dominus; et si in peccatis sit, remittentur ei. Confitemini ergo alterutrum peccata vestra, et orate pro invicem, ut salvemini."

Thus far the provision made by our merciful Lord for the remission of the sins of Christians, as disclosed explicitly or implicitly in the Holy Scriptures, according to the reading of the Catholic Church, has been explained. The reader may decide for himself if this doctrine is not in perfect harmony with those which have been previously exposed, and if it does not make a clear, intelligible sense of passages otherwise obscure and doubtful. A second sacrament, a "second plank after shipwreck," affords the means of returning to the state of grace in which the Christian man was first placed by baptism, and from which he has fallen by grievous sin, however numerous or enormous his crimes may have been. A complement to this sacrament has been provided in a third sacrament, intended for those who are in danger of death; which either restores them to life or fortifies them in the last struggle, as God sees to be most conducive to their salvation: by taking away the aggravation which sin lays upon bodily sickness with its special dangers to the soul, and strengthening the infirmity of nature which springs from the effects of sin.

There is another part of the Catholic doctrine respecting sin after baptism, however, which requires a brief elucidation. The church teaches, namely, that the sacrament of penance has not the same plenary efficacy for taking away sin and guilt from the penitent which baptism possesses. The penitent is not restored to the same degree of favor with God by sacramental absolution which he before enjoyed, nor is the penalty due to him fully remitted. Wherefore he must satisfy the justice of God: and if he passes out of this life with any debt to the divine justice resting upon him, he must remain in prison until that debt has been expiated by penal suffering. Closely connected with this is the doctrine that the same temporal punishment is also due to venial sins. I do not intend to dwell upon this point here. I will merely take a brief notice of the principal passages of the New Testament which sustain and confirm the Catholic doctrine of a purgatory after death, in which the soul is purified from the stains of sin which are found in it when it leaves the body in the state of grace, yet not entirely free from guilt.

The passage respecting the sin against the Holy Spirit cited above implies that some sins are remitted in the world to come, else the declaration made by our Lord, that this particular sin shall not be forgiven, " neither in this world, neither in the world to come," has no meaning. If a Catholic preacher should say: "There are men for whom, without a miracle of divine grace, there is no baptism, no penance, no purgatory, and thus no hope of salvation—such is their violent and obstinate hatred of the truth revealed by the Holy Spirit—but only eternal damnation, as the just punishment of final perseverance in sin"; such language would be perfectly in keeping with the known doctrine of the preacher and of the Catholic people to whom he was speaking. Other sinners, however grievously they have sinned, and however long they have put off repentance, may be, perhaps, baptized at the very hour of death, and go at once to heaven, as we frequently find to be the case. Or if they have been baptized, and can no more be washed in the laver of regeneration, they may be absolved, and in purgatory they may make satisfaction to God for the transgressions of their lives, so that eventually, being entirely purified from sin, they may enter heaven. The remission of sin in this world and in the world to come, in which the prayers for the dead and other works in aid of the faithful departed have a large share, is a familiar idea to a Catholic. And to be shut out even from purgatory, to be deprived of all aid from the prayers of the living after death, is the strongest expression to his mind of the hopelessness of an eternal doom.

There is another and a most remarkable passage in one of the Epistles to the Corinthians, in which, in figurative style, the apostle sets forth in a very terse and vivid manner the whole doctrine which I have just now stated in brief terms. " Other foundation can no man lay than that is laid, which is Jesus Christ. Now if any man build upon this foundation gold, silver, precious stones, wood, hay, stubble; every man's work shall be made manifest: for the day shall declare it, because it shall be revealed by fire; and the fire shall try every man's work of what sort it is. If any man's work abide which he hath built thereupon, he shall receive a reward. If any man's work shall be burned, he shall suffer loss: but he himself shall be saved; *yet so as by fire.*" *

Once more, St. Peter affirms that Christ "went and preached unto *the spirits in prison;* which sometime were disobedient, when once the long-suffering of God waited in the days of Noe. . . . For for this cause was the gospel preached also to them that are dead, that they might be judged according to men in the flesh, but live according to God in the spirit." †

This may suffice for the present, as a view of what Scripture teaches respecting the remission of sins after baptism. Its statements and allusions are more rare and indistinct on this topic than on those whose consideration has preceded. It may be accounted for in this way. The faithful to whom the epistles were addressed were recently baptized, and the catechumens or hearers to whom these epistles might be read, or who might hear the apostles preach, were unbaptized. In their first fervor and devotion the faithful had little need to be instructed respecting the sacrament of penance, and the rest had nothing to do with this sacrament at all. After baptism and confirmation, the most important sacrament to those early Christians was the Holy Communion. They were in the habit of attending at the

---

* 1 Cor. iii. 11-15. † 1 Peter iii. 19, 20; iv. 6.

divine oblation every morning, and of receiving the sacrament daily or weekly. Therefore, as was quite natural, the apostles spoke more frequently and explicitly about the Holy Communion than about any other sacrament, baptism alone excepted.

Let us recall the principles already established, in order to make the connection and end of our discourse more obvious. We are endeavoring to trace out the way of salvation as laid down in the New Testament. I have already proved that the sinner disposed by faith and repentance is placed in the state of grace and salvation through the sacrament of baptism; that he is made just and holy by a real and inherent sanctity; that he is to keep and increase this sanctity, and reduce it to act in his life, by keeping the commandments of God, which are prescribed to him as the condition of the favor of God and eternal life. I have also proved that the sacramental principle contained in the institution of baptism as the gate of entrance to eternal life must run through the whole order of grace, and manifest itself in other sacraments, in which the Christian may find the graces necessary for the full completion of that regenerate nature which is imparted in baptism. The regenerate man, being obliged to live a life wholly supernatural, to perform works above the powers of human nature, to overcome many and great temptations, to endure many trials, to work out his salvation in fear and trembling, and all this in a frail and corruptible body which is a heavy weight on the soul, needs some heavenly aliment to sustain him. He needs a perpetual source of sacramental grace, from which he can derive sustenance, vigor, healing virtue, and divine consolation, that he may grow and thrive, and be strengthened to avoid sin, to do good works, and to win eternal life. This sacrament has been provided in the Holy Eucharist, as the inspired scriptures of the New Testament most plainly teach.

Our Lord himself, as we are informed by his beloved apostle St. John in the sixth chapter of his gospel, taught the disciples that they were to live by a continual communication of virtue from his own sacred humanity: "I am the living bread which came down from heaven: if any man eat of this bread, he shall live for ever. . . . Verily, verily, I say unto you, except ye eat the flesh of the Son of man, and drink his blood, ye have no life in you. . . . He that eateth my flesh, and drinketh my blood, dwelleth in me, and I in him. As the living Father hath sent me, and I live by the Father: so he that eateth me, even he shall live by me."* At the last supper, when he had instituted and consecrated the Holy Eucharist, he gave holy communion to the apostles, saying:

---

* St. John vi. 51, *et seq*.

"This is my body which is given for you. . . . This cup is the new testament in my blood, which is shed for you."* And St. Paul writes to the Corinthians: "The cup of blessing which we bless, is it not the communion of the blood of Christ? The bread which we break, is it not the communion of the body of Christ?" Precisely because this food and drink is the sustenance and aliment of the life of the soul when it is received worthily, he ascribes to its unworthy reception the fact which he deplores, that "many are weak and sickly among you, and many sleep."† The perfect clearness and explicitness of these and similar statements make all comment and elaborate exposition unnecessary. It is not my object to prove the real presence, transubstantiation, or the sacrifice of the Mass. It is enough to show that the grace proceeding from the Mediator, Jesus Christ, for sustaining and invigorating the regenerate nature which he imparts in baptism, is conveyed through the sacrament of the Holy Eucharist. The express and full elucidation of the nature and effects of this sacrament can be found in the many excellent treatises which have been published on this special topic.

Nor is it necessary to speak particularly of the remaining sacraments which have not been noticed, to wit, Holy Order and Matrimony. The first of

---

* St. Luke xxii. 19, 20.   † 1 Cor. x. 16, xi. 30.

these is intended for the consecration and sanctification of those who are set apart to the sacred ministry of the word and sacraments and the government of the church. The second is for the sanctification of the conjugal and parental state in respect to the supernatural end of the family in the order of grace and salvation. It is, moreover, equally superfluous to prove the efficacy of prayer as a most certain means of grace and perseverance, since those who may be supposed to read these pages are already fully convinced of this truth, and well instructed in regard to the same.

I have shown what I proposed and promised to show at the outset: that salvation is provided for all men in Jesus Christ; that faith and repentance are the conditions for being placed in the state and in the way of salvation; that the instrument of regeneration is baptism; that salvation is actually attained by obedience to the law of Christ; and that special means are provided by which a Christian is strengthened and efficaciously aided to fulfil this obedience, to obtain pardon when he transgresses, and to attain the perfect and spotless sanctity which will entitle and fit him to enter the celestial kingdom. It is evident, therefore, that the whole work of salvation is comprised essentially in the fulfilment of the following conditions: to repent, to believe, to be baptized, to keep the commandments, to do penance if one has sinned, to receive worthily the sacraments, especially the Holy Eucharist, to undergo purgation after death, if one is not free from all guilt and stain. These conditions are not all necessary for all persons. That which is alone subjectively necessary and indispensable to the salvation of a soul is the absence of original and actual sin, and the presence of sanctifying grace. Therefore the only condition requisite for the salvation of an infant is that it be regenerated. The baptized child who attains the use of reason has no need of the conditions required of an adult person as the predisposition for baptism. If he commits no mortal sin, he has no need of repentance and penance in the strict sense of the words. If he is free from every stain at the hour of death, he has no need of purgatory. For the infant, sanctifying grace; for the adult, in addition to habitual grace, an actual faith informed by love and producing the fruit of good works, is therefore the inherent quality which justifies, and, when perfect, justifies completely. But that this indispensable condition may be verified in particular persons, according to their state and circumstances, the other conditions specified, in so far as they are possible and requisite, must be fulfilled. Therefore I have called them essential conditions, because they are all the conditions which constitute the essence of the way of salvation as a provision for all men under all varieties of state and circumstances. If these are all the conditions, they are the only conditions, and there can be no other conditions separate in their nature from these, or not in some way included or implied in them, or following necessarily from them. Nevertheless, this is not the complete account of the matter, but there still remains something which is, as it were, the substratum of these conditions, and necessary to their existence and fulfilment. This is the one true church established by Jesus Christ, in which his faith, his law, his sacraments, have their subsistence, and in which alone the individual Christian can comply with the conditions requisite for his salvation.

In the order of nature it is only necessary for the individual life, health, and perfection of each separate human being that he should be born, possess the means of sustenance, growth, health, activity, in his animal and rational nature, observe the natural laws, and direct his actions to the end prefixed by his Creator. But these are all impossible for him, except as a member of the human species, as a unit in a multitude of similar beings, having the same origin and bound together in a society by common laws. The unity and organic principles of the human race are the substratum of the life and well-being of each individual. It is the same in the order of grace. The church is the regenerated human species under its head, Jesus Christ, the second Adam; the divine society of true believers and subjects of the Redeemer of mankind; and it is only as a member of this society that the individual Christian is constituted in his supernatural personality with the rights and privileges of a Christian, and the ability to work out his own salvation by his own free acts concurring with the grace of God. This is one of the most important topics I have to treat of; in fact, the one which includes and involves all the rest. I shall therefore devote all the remaining part of this treatise to its thorough and ample explication.

CHAPTER FIFTH

Of the Church—Its Unity and Authority—Of the Rule of Faith—The Mystics—Luther's Doctrine of Private Illumination—Of Teaching Authority in General—Of Infallibility—Various Theories Examined and Tested—The Validity of the Argument from Scripture Established—Indirect, Negative, Cumulative, and Presumptive Proofs that the Catholic Church alone is the True Church.

THE proposition which I intend to prove, and to prove fundamentally and principally from the Holy Scripture, is, that God has established, as the necessary means of the salvation of the human race, a society which in its nature is one and universal—that is, a catholic church; and that it is in itself necessary, and both as a consequence from this necessity, and by a positive divine precept, strictly and indispensably obligatory on each individual to be a member of this church, in order to his salvation. This is a proposition which those Protestants who are called orthodox cannot deny to be true in a general sense. But I intend to prove that it is not only true in this sense, but also in the strict, proper, and specifically Catholic sense; and by means of it to identify the one true church established by Jesus Christ, into which every man is bound to enter in order to attain salvation.

This supernatural society, one and universal in its essence, was instituted at the same time that the human race was created. Adam and Eve were bound together by a supernatural as well as a natural bond which made them one in the Son of God, by the grace of a divine filiation to the Father, in the Holy Spirit. The entire human race existed in them, not actually, but potentially, as the parents and heads of all mankind, not only in respect to the order of generation and natural life, but also of regeneration and supernatural life. According to the primitive order of original justice, human society would have been a spiritual, a political, and a social organization all in one; the church, the state, the family, being distinct, but not separate, with one religion, one law, one language, and perpetual peace uniting all mankind in one common family whose father was God. This order was broken up by the sin of our first parents, who forfeited the right of transmitting regeneration to their posterity, together with the forfeiture of their own personal rights as children of God. This order being, however, restored in Christ, the second Adam, the regenerate and spiritual society of men under his headship must necessarily have been restored. Moreover, as his work was one both of rebuilding a ruined world, and of perpetual warfare against a hostile power and kingdom which had gained a footing on the earth, it was necessary that the organization, laws, and whole exterior discipline of this society should receive a higher degree of unity, strength and force, than that which was possessed by the original society. And as it was developed, extended, and engaged in more vast works and a more arduous warfare in the progress of ages and the continued evolution of the destinies of man toward their consummation, it would require an increasing consolidation, a more compact unity and force, an augmentation both of its power of resistance and its power of aggression. So long as the human race was restricted within the bounds of one family, the church was not distinct from the family; and so long as human society was composed of an aggregation of closely-related families under a patriarchal organization, the church was identical with this patriarchal state, until the apostasy of a large part of mankind from the true religion or bond of unity broke up the first state of society and brought on the Deluge. This same patriarchal order was renewed in the family of Noah, but very soon gave place to the breaking-up of the human race into separate tribes and nations. Unity of language, of religion, of laws, of sentiments, and of ends, was lost among mankind as a universal society, and henceforth was restricted within the sphere of one nation, until the time of the advent of the Redeemer. The calling of Abraham inaugurated the new dispensation of Israel, and the divine legation of Moses, the forerunner and type of Christ, gave it an organic law. All this was only prefatory to the foundation of the Catholic Church by Jesus Christ, the Redeemer and Restorer of mankind. The end of the redemption wrought out by Jesus Christ is the restoration of the human race to the unity of the supernatural order in God. The means by which this restoration is effected is the church, the last and most highly-organized institution which God has established for the consummation of the final end for which he has created the world. It must therefore contain within itself all those principles and forces which produce unification in the most perfect manner, both intensively and extensively, and its operation must consequently exhibit both the intensity and the extension of these forces in a manifest and visible unity of the highest degree and the most universal dominion.

In order to understand this fully it is necessary to premise some explanation of the nature of unity in general, and of the unity of the supernatural order in particular. Unity is defined by St. Thomas to be undivided being, to which, in respect to other beings, must be added, which is divided from all others. The most perfect unity is that of a simple essence, which is undivided and indivisible. The highest kind of indivisibility belongs to that essence which is the most absolutely simple or free from all composition whatever, which is the invisible and ineffable essence of God. In him alone, therefore, is absolute, essential unity, and in the world of created beings, the highest kind of unity is found only in spirits, whose nature is not divisible into parts, but is simple substance. Unity in plurality exists absolutely and perfectly only in God, who is One Essence in Three Persons. In this Trinity of Persons there is no real distinction between the Essence and the Persons, for the Infinite Being whom we call by the name of God is the Three Persons, Father, Son, and Holy Ghost; wherefore these three names denote, not a distinction of essence, but only of personality—a mystery which is entirely above our reason. Next in order to this perfect unity of essence in a plurality of persons is the unity of person in a duality of natures, or what is called the hypostatic union of the human with the divine nature in the person of our Lord Jesus Christ. In pure creatures the highest and most perfect union with God to which they can be raised is one which leaves them not only in their own distinct nature, but also in their distinct personality. Each one of these elevated creatures is a being in himself, with his own complete unity by which he is undivided in his own subsistence, and divided from all others; that is to say, exists as a separate individual. His union with God is a participation in a limited degree in that light and love which are the life of God, communicated to him by the Divine Spirit. The common participation of this life by a multitude of distinct persons constitutes their mutual union with each other in one society; that is, they are united together by a common beatific knowledge and love of God, necessarily producing a perfect love toward one another. This society is what is called the church triumphant, whose members are the blessed angels and men who are in heaven, and whose Head is Jesus Christ, in whom all are one in God.

Those who are on the way to this beatific union must necessarily partake in it in a manner suited to the prefatory state in which they are. They must be united with God through Jesus Christ, and united with all those who are thus united with God, by some participation of the divine light and love, which is the beginning of that which is made perfect in the celestial beatitude. This incipient beatitude and inchoate principle of union with God is that faith which is informed by love. God and the Saints in heaven are one in the beatific vision. This is essentially a spiritual and intellectual union, having its seat in the purely spiritual essence of God, and in the highest, most spiritual, most simple element of the rational nature of the beatified man or angel. The same principle of unity and order, however, extends itself throughout every part of the universe, and binds all together in one whole. This order and harmony is subordinate to the glorification and beatification of the saints, and ministers to its completion. In a like manner the kingdom of God on earth is, in the highest part of its essence, spiritual; and its inward, organic principle is a spiritual bond which binds together the children of God on earth in a spiritual union, which is the beginning of the perfect union of heaven. All external means, all institutions, all organization, in the visible and sensible order, are conditions, means, effects, or in some way subordinate parts of this unity, the soul of which is the grace of the Holy Spirit, and whose vital movements are faith, hope, and charity. This entire, composite whole constitutes the church militant on earth, the society of the faithful which is one and universal, or a universal unity.

The explanations already made of the nature of unity are sufficient to make it clearly intelligible that this universal unity is something different from the unity of a single individual; that it exists without any prejudice to the separate individual existence of the parts composing it; and that it has a true objective reality, not one which is merely in name or in the conception of the mind. The foundation of it has been pointed out in the unity in plurality which exists in the Being of God, who is one in Three Persons. The universal unity which unites the whole multitude of distinct, separate individuals who compose the supernatural society into one church, triumphant, suffering, and militant, is an imitation of the unity in Trinity, and of the hypostatic union of two natures in the One Person of Jesus Christ. The name *universal*, explained according to its etymology, expresses the whole notion of all the universals, and of the universal church specifically. It is *unum versus alia*— that which is one in respect to divers things. It denotes that unity which has an aptitude or capability of existing in many things. For instance, let us take the essence of finite spiritual being. It consists in intelligence, and exists by the creative act of God in all created spirits, however numerous they may be. It is their common nature, by virtue of which they are capable of society with each other, through a mutual communication and concurrence of thought and of consequent volition, and are separated from any similar society with any inferior natures by an impassable chasm. In pure spirits the power and act of intelligence are determined to a specific nature and operation which is simply and exclusively intellectual. As purely intellectual beings, the angels are therefore by their nature capable of a more perfect society with one another than with any intelligent nature of an inferior order. In the human species intelligent spirit exists in the form of a soul which is rational in distinction from the purely intellectual nature of the angel, and determined by its specific essence to be the form—that is, the vital principle—of a body. Man is a rational animal; and, as such, he is by nature capable of a more perfect society with those of his own species than with those of any other. The essence of humanity is composed of two constituent parts, animality and rationality. This specific essence is a universal; it is a one, which has an aptitude to exist in many, and can be multiplied in an indefinite number of separate individuals. When it is produced into actual being, the composition of the essence with existence makes the individual man. All individual men, therefore, bear a perfect similitude to each other in respect to all that which constitutes them human beings, so that there lies in their very nature an aptitude for society with each other, and an inclination to this society or to common social occupations and enjoyments. But this is not the only bond of unity and brotherhood among men. The unity of the species, which includes the generic reason making man an animal, with the specific reason which makes him rational, is a unity which not only gives to all men a similitude of nature, but also a common origin and a blood-relationship. Man belongs to that order of beings which are multiplied by generation. And whatever may be the case with inferior species of animals or with plants, it is certainly a revealed fact, supported by all the scientific evidence accessible to us, that all men are descended from one pair of parents. There is, therefore, a natural society, constituted by the very creation of the first man and the first woman, from which the whole human race derives its existence, and of which each man is necessarily by his birth made a member for life. The family, the primordial social unit, is a necessary condition of human existence and welfare. It is not needful to show the natural and necessary development of the family into the more extensive societies in which men have always been associated together. Enough has been said to prove that men cannot exist or attain any natural and rational end of their existence in a state of mere individuality and singularity. As an intelligent creature each man is necessarily a partaker in that common, spiritual nature which makes one order in the universe, to which all intelligent creatures belong. As one of the lowest grade in this order, that of rational animals, he is necessarily a partaker in the common nature of humanity, and one individual of a species derived by generation from its first progenitors. As a child he is one of a family which, if lawfully constituted, originates in a stable and permanent union of his parents in marriage. In his other relations he is one among many bound together in society by various common ends and common laws.

In the order of regeneration, or the supernatural order, the same principles which lie at the base of the natural order under which the intelligent creation is constituted are elevated to a higher plane, but remain substantially the same. The unity of the essence of intelligent beings is the reason of their capacity to be elevated to a higher common plane in the supernatural order, and to share together in a common beatitude in the vision of God. In this higher order the intellectual and rational natures are also brought nearer together and united in a more perfect society with each other. The human nature, in the Person of the Eternal Word, is elevated above the angelic by virtue of the hypostatic union. In the persons of glorified men it is made, by adoption, equal to the angelic. Angels and men form one perfect society or kingdom of heaven by their subjection to one Sovereign, Jesus Christ, by their filiation to One Father, God, by their communication in one intellectual act, the vision of the Divine Essence in Three Persons, by the possession of one supreme good, by unity of will, by perpetual and perfect mutual love, by being made, each and every one, a part of a grand, symmetrical whole, a single masterpiece of divine art in a grand gallery of celestial, spiritual beauty, to the praise and glory of the infinite Creator, who is their archetype. The supernatural being which is given them, whose last complement is the light of glory by which they are made capable of receiving the beatific intuition of God, although not a new essence, is nevertheless a new determination of the intelligent power to an act infinitely above its nature. It is sanctifying grace which is the elevating principle, or rather, which contains within itself the elevating principle, and constitutes the new quality of the ennobled nature. Sanctifying grace effects the actual union of the elevated nature with God in the Person of the Word, by a kind of participation of the hypostatic union of created with uncreated being in Jesus Christ, who is God and man. We may call it, therefore, in a certain way, the *differentia* of a new, supernatural species, which includes under itself all the genera and species of intelligent creatures which are known to us—that is, all angels and men, in so far as these are raised to a supernatural state. As all angels are made angels by participating in the angelic, intellectual nature, and all men are made men by participating in human nature, so all the sons of God are made sons of God by participating in sanctifying grace. The elevated or regenerate nature is a universal, or a one which has aptitude to exist in many spiritual genera, species, and individuals. Those who have it in its proper actuality as sanctifying grace, and only those, whether they are in heaven, in purgatory, or on the earth, constitute that spiritual society in union with God which is called, in the highest sense of that word, the church of Jesus Christ; and of these, only such as actually attain the state of glory constitute the perfect and everlasting church, or kingdom of heaven. There is, however, a temporary union with the church, and also one which is partial and imperfect, during the period of its formation; so that in its more extensive sense the church is a society including many members who become finally reprobates, and many who are not in the state of grace. The union of the beatified with God is perfect and indissoluble. The union of the unbeatified, who are in the inchoate order of grace which is a medium between the state of nature and the state of supernatural glory, is imperfect, and in its nature dissoluble. It has, moreover, its grades of relative perfection, and its own particular conditions, suited to an inchoate and intermediate order. Its essence is therefore modified, and various accidents are added to it, qualifying its state and condition as it actually exists and operates during the state of probation on the earth. The church, as one and universal, in respect to that collection of individuals who are its members on the earth, must, therefore, possess in addition to its essential and eternal principle of unity, another which is inherent in it, and which is the principle of an accidental and temporary unity. The church universal on the earth has in its very nature the oneness *per se*, which has been already explained, in which each individual participates, and which has its living, active operation in faith, hope, and charity. It has also a oneness *per accidens*, which consists in an exterior, visible organization and order, containing all the means and institutions, all the instruments and laws—in a word, all the complex arrangement of second causes which is necessary to produce, extend, increase, and perpetuate, through the power communicated and concurring of the Spirit of God, the regeneration of men and their union with God by faith, hope, and charity. This unity is not called *per accidens* because it is something fortuitous or unnecessary. It is not the accidental unity of a mere heap of stones, which is only a unity of aggregation, but a unity of order, "which consists in this: that a number of distinct parts are bound together by an intelligent cause according to a fixed plan, in such a manner that in their connection they form an organic whole."* The unity of a building, of a university, of an army, is a unity of this kind. It is called *per accidens*, because the union of parts is produced by an extrinsic, and not an intrinsic, cause. This particular accidental unity of the church of which I am speaking is also accidental in respect to its essential being, inasmuch as it is something which *accedes* to it, or is superadded, in order that it may exercise its proper operation with perfection.

Thus far I have been reasoning from principles derived partly from reason and partly from revelation, without adducing direct proofs from the Scripture. But in great part I have stated what is admitted as true by standard Protestant authors, and specifically by Calvinists, and I have been only preparing the way for a right understanding of my proposition respecting the church, and of the proofs which I intend to bring forward. But before I proceed with the main argument, I will first cite a few of the passages of Holy Scripture in which are contained the several principal doctrinal statements which I have made as preliminary to the doctrine of the divine constitution of the catholic church militant.

" Jesus saith unto him, Have I been so long time with you, and yet hast thou not known me, Philip? he that hath seen me hath seen the Father. . . .

---
* Stöckl, " Lehrb. der Phil. Ontol.," sec. 97.

Believest thou not that I am in the Father, and the Father in me? . . . And I will pray the Father, and he shall give you another Comforter, that he may abide with you for ever; the Spirit of truth; . . . for he dwelleth with you, and shall be in you. . . . And this is life eternal, that they might know thee the only true God.* . . . Neither pray I for these alone, but for them also which shall believe on me through their word; that they all may be one; as thou, Father, art in me, and I in thee, that they also may be one in us. . . . And the glory which thou gavest me I have given them; that they may be one, even as we are one: I in them, and thou in me, that they may be made perfect in one. . . . Father, I will that they also, whom thou hast given me, be with me where I am; that they may behold my glory, which thou hast given me: for thou lovedst me before the foundation of the world." †

"For through him we both have access by one Spirit unto the Father. Now therefore ye are no more strangers and foreigners, but fellow-citizens with the saints, and of the household of God; and are built upon the foundation of the apostles and prophets, Jesus Christ himself being the chief corner-stone; in whom all the building fitly framed together groweth unto a holy temple in the Lord: in

---

* St. John xiv. 9, 10, 16, 17; xvii. 3.   † *Ibid.* xvii. 20-24.

whom ye also are builded together for a habitation of God through the Spirit. . . . The fellowship of the mystery, which from the beginning of the world hath been hid in God, who created all things by Jesus Christ: to the intent that now unto the principalities and powers in heavenly places might be known by the church the manifold wisdom of God. . . . For this cause I bow my knees unto the Father of our Lord Jesus Christ, of whom the whole family in heaven and earth is named. . . . Unto him be glory in the church by Christ Jesus throughout all ages, world without end. . . . I therefore, the prisoner of the Lord, beseech you that ye walk worthy of the vocation wherewith ye are called, . . . endeavoring to keep the unity of the Spirit in the bond of peace. There is one body, and one Spirit, even as ye are called in one hope of your calling; one Lord, one faith, one baptism, one God and Father of all, who is above all, and through all, and in you all. But unto every one of us is given grace according to the measure of the gift of Christ. . . . For the perfecting of the saints, for the work of the ministry, for the edifying of the body of Christ: till we all come in the unity of the faith, and of the knowledge of the Son of God, unto a perfect man, unto the measure of the stature of the fulness of Christ." *

* Ephesians ii. 18-22; iii. 9-11, 14, 15, 21; iv. 1, 3-7, 12, 13.

"God, who at sundry times and in divers manners spake in time past unto the fathers by the prophets, hath in these last days spoken unto us by his Son, whom he hath appointed heir of all things, by whom also he made the worlds; who being the brightness of his glory, and the express image of his person, and upholding all things by the word of his power, when he had by himself purged our sins, sat down on the right hand of the Majesty on high; being made so much better than the angels, as he hath by inheritance obtained a more excellent name than they. . . . Are they not all ministering spirits, sent forth to minister to them who shall be heirs of salvation? . . . For unto the angels hath he not put in subjection the world to come, whereof we speak. But one in a certain place testified, saying, What is man, that thou art mindful of him? or the son of man, that thou visitest him? Thou madest him a little lower than the angels; thou crownedst him with glory and honor, and didst set him over the works of thy hands; thou hast put all things in subjection under his feet. . . . But now we see not yet all things put under him. But we see Jesus, who was made a little lower than the angels for the suffering of death, crowned with glory and honor."*

"Giving thanks unto the Father, which hath

* Hebrews c.c. i., ii.

made us meet to be partakers of the inheritance of the saints in light; who hath delivered us from the power of darkness, and hath translated us into the kingdom of his dear Son: . . . who is the image of the invisible God, the first-born of every creature: for by him were all things created, that are in heaven, and that are in earth, visible and invisible, whether they be thrones, or dominions, or principalities, or powers: all things were created by him, and for him: and he is before all things, and by him all things consist. And he is the head of the body, the church: who is the beginning, the first-born from the dead: that in all things he might have the pre-eminence. For it pleased the Father that in him should all fulness dwell; and, having made peace through the blood of his cross, by him to reconcile all things unto himself; by him, I say, whether they be things in earth, or things in heaven. . . . And ye are complete in him, which is the head of all principality and power: . . buried with him in baptism, wherein also ye are risen with him. . . . If ye then be risen with Christ, . . . your life is hid with Christ in God. When Christ, who is our life, shall appear, then shall ye also appear with him in glory. . . . Ye have put off the old man with his deeds; and have put on the new man, which is renewed in knowledge after the image of him that created him. . . . Put on therefore, as the elect of God, . . . charity which is the bond of perfectness. And let the peace of God rule in your hearts, to the which also ye are called in one body." *

" Now there are diversities of gifts, but the same Spirit. And there are differences of administrations, but the same Lord. And there are diversities of operations, but it is the same God which worketh all in all. . . . But all these worketh that one and the self-same Spirit, dividing to every man severally as he will. For as the body is one, and hath many members, and all the members of that one body, being many, are one body: so also is Christ. For by one Spirit we are all baptized into one body, . . . and have been made to drink into one spirit. . . . And yet shew I unto you a more excellent way. . . . Charity never faileth: but whether there be prophecies they shall fail; whether there be tongues, they shall cease; whether there be knowledge, it shall vanish away. For we know in part, and we prophesy in part. But when that which is perfect is come, then that which is in part shall be done away. . . . For now we see through a glass, darkly; but then face to face: now I know in part; but then shall I know even as also I am known. And now abideth faith, hope, charity, these three; but the greatest of these is

* Coloss. i. 12–20; ii. 10, 12; iii, 1–4, 9, 10, 12, 14, 15.

charity. . . . For as in Adam all die, even so in Christ shall all be made alive. But every man in his own order: Christ the first-fruits; afterward they that are Christ's at his coming. Then cometh the end, when he shall have delivered up the kingdom to God, even the Father; when he shall have put down all rule and all authority and power. For he must reign, till he hath put all enemies under his feet. . . . And when all things shall be subdued unto him, then shall the Son also himself be subject unto him that put all things under him, that God may be all in all." *

"Blessed be the God and Father of our Lord Jesus Christ, who hath blessed us with all spiritual blessings in heavenly places in Christ, . . . having made known unto us the mystery of his will, . . . that in the fulness of times he might gather together in one all things in Christ, both which are in heaven, and which are on earth; . . . according to the working of his mighty power, which he wrought in Christ, when he raised him from the dead, and set him at his own right hand in the heavenly places, far above all principality, and power, and might, and dominion, and every name that is named, not only in this world, but also in that which is to come: and hath put all things under his feet, and gave him to be the head over all things to

* 1 Cor. xii. 4-13, 31; xiii. 8-13; xv. 22-28.

the church, which is his body, the fulness of him that filleth all in all." *

" For ye are not come unto the mount that might be touched. . . . But ye are come unto Mount Sion, and unto the city of the living God, the heavenly Jerusalem, and to an innumerable company of angels, to the general assembly and church of the first-born, which are written in heaven, and to God the Judge of all, and to the spirits of just men made perfect, and to Jesus the mediator of the new covenant, and to the blood of sprinkling, that speaketh better things than the blood of Abel. . . . . Whose voice then shook the earth: but now he hath promised, saying, Yet once more I shake not the earth only, but also heaven. And this word, Yet once more, signifieth the removing of those things that are shaken, as of things that are made, that those things which cannot be shaken may remain. Wherefore we receiving a kingdom which cannot be moved, let us have grace, whereby we may serve God acceptably with godly fear." †

"And I appoint unto you a kingdom, as my Father hath appointed unto me; that ye may eat and drink at my table in my kingdom, and sit on thrones judging the twelve tribes of Israel." ‡

" He was taken up, after that he through the Holy

---

* Eph. i. 3, 9, 10, 19–23.   † Heb. xii. 18–28.
‡ St. Luke xxii. 29, 30.

Ghost had given commandments unto the apostles whom he had chosen: to whom also he had showed himself alive after his passion by many infallible proofs, being seen of them forty days, and speaking of the things pertaining to the kingdom of God: and, being assembled together with them, commanded them that they should not depart from Jerusalem, but wait for the promise of the Father, which, saith he, ye have heard of me. For John truly baptized with water; but ye shall be baptized with the Holy Ghost not many days hence. When they therefore were come together, they asked of him, saying, Lord, wilt thou at this time restore again the kingdom to Israel? And he said unto them, It is not for you to know the times or the seasons, which the Father hath put in his own power. But ye shall receive power, after that the Holy Ghost is come upon you." *

That the apostles, after they had "received power," did found a visible Christian church, with a clergy, sacraments, government, public worship, and at least one holyday, is believed by all orthodox Protestants. They all believe in some sense that article of the Creed, "the Holy, Catholic Church." Even Congregationalists or Independents admit that there is a certain type or form of outward, visible organization, according to which all particular

* Acts i. 2–8.

churches ought to be constituted, and that all these ought to be united together in mutual fellowship and communion. It is not necessary, therefore, to prove that there is a visible church which is the ordinary means of salvation, or to prove the importance and obligation of some kind of unity binding together all the members of this church.

The point to be proved is that the visible church is constituted in a strict organic unity, as one society, one kingdom, one body, undivided in itself and divided from all other societies, unchangeable, perpetual, exclusive, sovereign—a church, "one, holy, catholic, and apostolic," in the strict Catholic sense as distinguished from each and every Protestant variation.

I shall prove this, first, by deduction from what has been already proved. It has been proved that grace is conferred through sacraments, which cannot be lawfully and efficaciously received except on condition of certain dispositions respecting both faith and morals; and that the state of grace itself exacts the fulfilment of a certain fixed law of religion and morality, in which true Christian and justifying righteousness essentially consists, and through which heaven is to be obtained as its due reward. Now, these things cannot exist with certainty and stability; except in a perfectly-organized society, in which there is a sovereign authority determining faith, discipline, and morals; without a perpetual miracle. Nothing can be more obvious than this must be to any one who will reflect on it attentively.

First, in respect to the sacraments themselves; their number, their nature, the conditions of their valid and lawful administration, must be certainly defined, and provision must be made for their reception by all persons, everywhere, and through all time, who are desirous of receiving them and are properly disposed. All this requires that authority to teach, to make laws, to judge and decide upon all questions and all cases arising out of the administration of the sacraments, should be delegated by God to certain persons. This authority must extend over the whole church and all its members throughout the world and until the end of time. It will be sufficient to show this more minutely in respect to one sacrament only—the sacrament of baptism. First, as to the ministers of the sacrament. As it is a sacrament of initiation into the church, the right to administer it must be confided to certain persons having authority to examine and instruct candidates, to judge of their qualification for membership, and to give them legal admission. These persons must be designated by a fixed and uniform law, and there can be no law without legislators and judges, without subordination of inferior to superior tribunals, or without one supreme authority and tribunal of the last resort. If there is dispute and dissension concerning the persons who are competent to give baptism validly and lawfully in the name of Christ, doubt and uncertainty are thrown upon the true way of salvation at its very entrance. How can one know whether he has received the real sacrament or not, unless there is a judgment, pronounced by a supreme tribunal established by Jesus Christ himself, declaring what persons are capable of administering the sacrament validly? A Catholic knows that any person whosoever can administer the sacrament validly, however irregular or unlawful his act may be. But he knows this only by the judgment of the Holy See. A Protestant cannot know whether lay baptism or the baptism of a schismatical minister is valid or invalid, nor can he even know what is necessary to make a man a real minister of Jesus Christ. The validity of sacraments administered in schism and heresy was denied by St. Cyprian and many others before the Roman Church finally decided the question. The validity of any baptism not administered by a bishop, priest, or deacon, who has received true episcopal ordination, is denied by a number of learned Anglicans.

The necessary matter and form of the sacrament is another question of equal importance, which has caused a great schism among Protestants, and which cannot be decided without the judgment of a supreme tribunal which all Christians are bound to obey.

The subjects capable of receiving baptism must also be determined. Are infants and idiots capable or incapable subjects? Are persons who are baptized without the required inward dispositions validly baptized or not? And what are they to do, in order to rectify the wrong they have done to themselves and to God by receiving a sacrament in a sacrilegious manner?

There are, moreover, other matters to be determined which respect, not the essence of the sacrament and the conditions of its validity, but its regular and lawful administration. It is evident that only those lawfully authorized by Jesus Christ have the right to administer the sacrament, whatever may be the case respecting the validity of the act when performed by other persons. It is equally evident that it must be a sin to receive baptism from any person who is not lawfully authorized to administer it. And this law, again, presupposes a tribunal and a judge having a supreme and universal authority over the whole church, both clergy and people. Without it endless dissensions and schisms must occur, as is seen from the history of all sects which have separated from the Roman Church.

The dispositions which are requisite in adult catechumens, and the obligations which all baptized persons contract in the sacrament, make it still more manifest that the church must be constituted in a strict organic unity under a supreme authority.

These dispositions and obligations relate, in the first place, to faith. A catechumen must believe in the doctrines revealed by God through the prophets and apostles, as a condition of receiving baptism worthily. He must learn these doctrines from some certain and authentic source. The church is the judge of the correctness and sufficiency of his faith, and must therefore possess a standard and rule of faith which is explicit and invariable, and have a magistracy committed to certain authorized teachers and judges, who must be the same persons who are authorized to admit candidates into the church through baptism. These persons are, of course, the pastors and clergy of the church. And, as they are necessarily very numerous, it is impossible that they should be kept to a correct standard and rule of teaching and judgment without an authority of superior over inferior pastors, who are relatively few in number, without tribunals regularly constituted, to which the pastors themselves are amenable, and without some supreme tribunal, whose jurisdiction is universal, by which the chief pastors themselves are regulated and kept to one uniform standard of doctrine.

The baptized person must continue to profess the true faith as a condition of receiving the other sacraments, remaining in the state of justification, and attaining salvation. He must educate his children in the same faith. He is responsible to the church, as well as to God, for the fulfilment of this obligation. The pastors of the church must, therefore, teach him sound doctrine, warn him against all errors in faith, watch over the instruction of his children, and exercise discipline over him if he goes astray—even, if necessary, excommunicate him. If there are diverse teachers, doctrines, and sects, each claiming to be true and to possess the right to his allegiance, he must follow the true pastor, the true doctrine, the true church. This teaching authority, this doctrine, this church, must be the one established by Jesus Christ, and the same in all times and places. There can be but one way of salvation for all men. But how can all men, everywhere, recognize it, unless its unity is visible, and one supreme doctrinal authority determines for the whole world which are the legitimate pastors who teach the true faith and govern the true church?

The second condition for a worthy reception of baptism is repentance for the sins which the person has committed, and a resolution to keep the whole law of God. A new obligation to keep the natural law springs out of the baptismal vows, and an obligation is contracted to keep the specifically Christian precepts. In respect to these moral duties the baptized person is responsible to the church, and amenable to her discipline. The church is, therefore, the judge of all ethical questions and relations, which are extremely numerous, minute, and complicated. How can the member of the church guide himself according to her true teaching in respect to morals, be secure against the danger of false teaching from his own particular pastors, or have any safeguard for his own rights of conscience against injustice and tyranny on their part, unless there is one supreme tribunal to which all alike are subject, and which establishes one uniform moral code throughout the whole church?

It is, moreover, evident that no merely external organization under a hierarchical government with one supreme head would be sufficient to secure unity in the true faith and doctrine, and the right administration of discipline, without the perpetual exercise of a supernatural providence over the church. The church must be governed by the Holy Spirit, and made indefectible and infallible, otherwise it is liable to become corrupt in doctrine and practice, and to lead men away from the faith and law of

Christ. This would be the destruction of the Way of Salvation provided by God for all mankind, and the construction of a new way to perdition. God could not permit this to take place. For, if he has constructed an ark in which he has commanded all men to embark, that they may pass over the sea of the world to the shore of eternal life, he must provide for the safe passage of the ark, and cannot permit it to be engulfed in the waves of the ocean.

A sincere and religious person, a Presbyterian for example, might here reply as follows: "I admit the necessity of a positive and certain rule of faith and practice, of belief in definitely and clearly proposed doctrines and obedience to fixed and well-known laws. I believe that God has really provided a Way of Salvation, which the soul that is guided by divine grace cannot mistake, in which it cannot err, and by which it walks securely to eternal life. I have that rule of faith in the Word of God contained in the Bible, and I have in the same a rule of life. This rule of faith has come to me through the church and the religious teachers under whose instruction I have been brought up. I do not pretend that they are infallible. But it is not necessary that they should be. It is sufficient that I have evidence that they do not actually err or deceive me in proposing to me the Scriptures. This evidence I have. Moreover, since the Word of God has come to me safely through their hands, I may presume that it is safe for me to receive the sacraments also from the same hands. Besides this, the interior light and consolation which I receive from the Holy Spirit, which I can no more distrust than I can distrust the light of reason and conscience, give me an assurance that I am safe and in the right way, and I am confirmed in this security by the agreement which I see existing among many persons who give evidence of being truly sanctified by the Holy Spirit, in the same doctrine and the same practice of religious observances which I have been taught, and which I believe to be right."

In replying to this plausible statement, which I believe to be a correct expression of the real mental attitude in which most of those who call themselves Evangelical Christians stand toward the Catholic Church, when they consider with any serious attention the call which she makes upon them to return to her bosom, I shall reserve the last part of it for separate examination. By this last part, I intend all that relates to the light of the Holy Spirit in the soul of the individual. The first part I shall refute by a process which may seem to be remote and indirect, but which I think will be found by any one who follows it patiently and attentively to be conclusive and satisfactory.

In the first place, then, I beg of my Presbyterian or Evangelical friend, who believes that he is in possession of what he is fond of calling "the whole counsel of God" in regard to the way of salvation, to enquire of himself how he originally acquired this conviction or belief. I refer now to that belief which he has had from his childhood, which pre-existed to that moment when he supposes that his justification took place, and which exists in those who give an intellectual assent to Evangelical doctrines. It is evident that he first believed these doctrines on the authority of his parents, and afterwards on that also of his religious teachers. This is the way established by God in the order of nature, and also in the order of grace. God has placed children under the tutelage of parents, and has implanted in their souls a disposition to believe and obey their teaching. Wherever any kind of organized religious or scientific instruction exists in the community, the children who are its recipients naturally and unavoidably submit to it with the same docility which their nature inclines them to exercise toward their parents. My Presbyterian friend will admit that God originally established this order as a secure and infallible method of instructing and directing the whole human race in all things relating both to their temporal and eternal welfare. Adam and Eve, in their primitive state, were qualified to instruct their children in all divine and human wisdom. If sin had never entered the world, all parents and elders would have been the successors of Adam and Eve in the same office and with the same perfect qualifications. The order of Providence respecting instruction which still exists in human nature is, therefore, something which has survived the fall, like marriage, and is a divine institution, impaired but not destroyed. So far as it exists in connection with the divine plan of redemption, it is an original institution of the primitive state restored. In its impaired and imperfect state it is evident that this institution can neither be so completely perverted as to become the means of teaching nothing but absolute falsehood, and prescribing nothing but that which is absolutely sinful, nor yet sufficient to teach the absolute truth and prescribe all that which is morally good without mixture of evil. In that proportion in which it approximates to the original institution of God, it must contain a greater amount of that truth and morality, which would have been transmitted in their integrity if the original state of mankind had continued in all its perfection. And in its restored condition it ought to be equivalent to what it was intended to remain in perpetuity, according to the first plan of God, **if our first parents had not sinned.** Therefore, in the case of those who are educated in every other religion or sect except in the true church, there must be a greater or lesser amount of truth taught them by their parents and other natural instructors, together with a lesser or greater amount of error. Now, as error cannot have any authority over the mind and conscience of a rational creature, it must be both the right and the duty of every man to reject that part of the instruction which he has received from his parents and elders which is erroneous, whenever he is reasonably convinced that it is erroneous, and to accept the truth which is presented to him from some other source. It is always possible for him to obtain this conviction, under every supposition but one, viz., that he has been educated under an infallible teaching, which has given him the pure and complete truth, unmixed with error.

Now, let us examine the principal gradations of religious teaching under which various classes of the human race are educated, and which our Presbyterian friend condemns as essentially erroneous or imperfect, until we come to his own doctrine; that we may see if the principle on which he condemns the one nearest to himself, and which is available for the condemnation of every lower one successively until we reach the lowest, is not of equal conclusiveness against his own position. Beginning at the lowest form of religion, heathenism, what argument would a philosophical and at the same time religiously orthodox Jew, who may be taken to represent both Theism, and Revealed Religion in its most general sense, employ, to convince an intelligent, upright pagan that he ought to believe in One God as revealed by the light of reason and the Old Testament? The argument will be one proving that the very principles and judgments of reason and conscience, as educated under the influence of his ancestral religion, require him to cast off every part of it which contradicts the doctrine of pure Monotheism. It will, moreover, prove to him that the Old Testament is an authentic record of a more ancient and universal history, tradition, law, than his own; of which his own is only a disfigured copy; and that it contains a revelation from God accredited by the most satisfactory and incontestable evidence.

In what manner will a Unitarian argue, in turn, with the Jew, to convince him of the truth of Christianity? He will show him that the divine mission of Jesus Christ is clearly proved by the Old Testament, and in various other ways will argue that Judaism has its proper development and completion in Christianity. All the motives of credibility which establish the truth of Judaism, therefore, prove equally the truth of Christianity.

The Unitarian, in turn, must answer for himself

to our Presbyterian friend. He will argue that Jesus Christ, the great Prophet and Teacher, sent from God to take up and complete the mission of Moses, taught his own true and proper divinity as a fundamental doctrine of the faith. Moreover, that he provided for the teaching of the faith to all nations by his apostles, whose writings contain the doctrines of the Trinity, Incarnation, Redemption, Original Sin, the necessity of regeneration and supernatural grace, and other doctrines, rejected by the Unitarian. He will argue, moreover, that it was the mission of Christianity to convert all nations to the knowledge and worship of the One True God; and that all Christians, except a handful, worship the One God in Three Persons, one of whom is the Lord Jesus Christ, God made Man, and crucified for us; hoping for salvation through his precious blood. Unitarians, therefore, have separated themselves from the mass of believers, have made for themselves a pseudo-Christianity, have renounced the genuine, authentic doctrine of Christ and the apostles, and are thus in flagrant contradiction to their profession of being followers and disciples of Jesus Christ. Even though the Unitarian should profess to believe the Bible as containing the pure and perfect revelation of divine truth, or even as being inspired in all its parts by the Spirit of God, the Presbyterian will tell him that this is of no avail to establish his character as a Christian, since he does not believe the true and real sense of the Bible, but his own false interpretation. As the principles which inform the natural reason and conscience of the pagan require him to believe in One God, the author of revelation; and as the principles of the Theist and the Jew require them to believe in the revelation made by Jesus Christ; so the principles and motives of credibility by which the Unitarian is convinced of the divine mission of Jesus Christ equally prove his true and proper divinity, the Trinity, and the whole body of doctrine contained and implied in the orthodox creed of the universal church.

Our Presbyterian friend must now face the arguments of one who stands in a higher grade than himself—that is, the advocate of a church professing to be founded on the apostolic succession of its bishops, and to be identical in constitution and doctrine with the apostolic church. Passing by the Protestant Episcopalian, we will bring forward the true, genuine High-Churchman—that is, the champion of the Greek Church. He will be able to prove to the Presbyterian that his sect has done precisely the same thing which he accuses the sect of Unitarians of having perpetrated. Professing to recognize the divine authority of Jesus Christ, it has rejected a large part of the doctrine which he has taught. It has rejected the polity, order, and teaching authority established at his command by the apostles. It has given a new and false sense to an essential part of the teaching of the Holy Scripture, and altogether rejected a large part of the true canon of Scripture as apocryphal. It has separated itself from the great body of Christian believers, denied a portion of the orthodox creed of the universal church, and mingled heresy with the remainder which it has retained. You have received, the Greek may say to the Presbyterian, your Bible and your interpretation of it, your mode of worship and your rule of life as a Christian, from the instruction of your parents and pastors, who have professed to teach you in the name of the church of Christ, and in the name of Christ himself. But go back a little, and you will find that your ancestors revolted from the instruction which they had received from the church in which they had been educated; which had come down from the teachers of their first Christian ancestors by whom they were converted to Christ; from the earliest ages, and from the founders of universal Christendom. From that ancient church you have received your canon of the New Testament, that part of the canon of the Old Testament which you retain, your creeds, your orthodox doctrine of the Trinity, the Incarnation, and whatever else you profess which is orthodox as opposed to the Arian, Sabellian, Nestorian, Eutychian, Monothelite, Pelagian, and Semipelagian heresies. Your General Assembly in the United States vindicated your orthodoxy before the Bishop of Rome, the primate of Christendom, on the plea that you accept the definitions of the first six Œcumenical Councils as a true testimony of the faith delivered to the church by the apostles. If their testimony to the doctrines of the orthodox and catholic creed respecting the Trinity and the Incarnation is worthy to be received; you have the same reason for receiving it, concerning that entire body of doctrine and that complete system of ecclesiastical polity which all the bishops and doctors of the age of these first councils, the very heretics whom they condemned and excommunicated assenting, declare to have been received from the apostles. The article of "The One, Holy, Catholic, and Apostolic Church" is as much a part of the Creed as the one which defines that Jesus Christ is "of one substance with the Father." The orthodox churches of Alexandria, Antioch, Jerusalem, Ephesus, Athens, and the other episcopal sees of the East, where St. Peter, St. Paul, St. Athanasius, St. John Chrysostom, preached and governed, have never changed their doctrine, their polity, their worship. But you have changed, founded a new church, invented a new religion, wholly diverse from that which existed throughout the Catholic Church before the East and the West were divided; and from that of every sect which has retained the episcopal succession, the priesthood, the sacrifice, the seven sacraments, and the outward semblance of conformity to the constitution of the church which the apostles established. Therefore, your claim to orthodoxy and your profession of following the doctrine and law of Christ and the apostles are futile, and your own principles require you to return to that catholic church which your forefathers abandoned.

All that the Greek can say to the Presbyterian can be with equal justice retorted upon himself. He is a schismatic. What he calls the Orthodox or Holy Eastern Church has not organic unity even in itself, but is an aggregation of independent churches without a head. It is not in communion with the great body of the bishops whose apostolic descent it recognizes. It has revolted against the Apostolic See, whose primacy its own formularies confess, and whose supreme authority its patriarchs recognized and obeyed while it was in unity with all catholic Christendom. It teaches the faith respecting the One, Catholic, and Apostolic Church, yet practically denies that the church exists on the earth; since it dare not assume to possess and exercise the functions of the catholic church in its separate state, and will not acknowledge the right of the true church to that august title and supreme power which really belong to her. The Greek schismatic, therefore, while he calls himself a Catholic, confesses that he adheres to a fragment which once made a portion of the Catholic Church. His boasted catholicity is but a theory which his practice contradicts. The admonition which he addresses to the Presbyterian falls with an inevitable and crushing rebound upon his own head.

There is, therefore, in every form of religious and moral instruction by authority, except that which is given by a supreme and infallible Teacher, a flaw which sooner or later betrays itself. Reason and conscience are awakened and in part instructed by this imperfect teaching. But they are awakened and instructed by a teaching which does not satisfy their demands, but causes them to long for a guide to lead them higher, and an instruction which is more complete and self-consistent. One who looks for truth by means of natural reason alone desires to find a perfect and complete philosophy. One who looks for the highest truth in a revelation from God desires to know that revelation certainly and completely, at least so far as it is necessary for his spiritual good. Moreover, reason and conscience cannot rightly and honorably subject themselves to any human instruction, except because and in so far as this instruction is reasonably considered as a mere instrument of God, whose mind alone is the measure of truth and his will of good. Why does the child reverence, believe, and obey his parents? He dimly apprehends in them a certain majesty, authority, and protecting love which he afterwards discovers to have their being in God. They represent God to him before he knows that God exists and made him. When his reason and conscience are developed, he knows that his duty to them is derived from, and measured by, his duty to God. The obligation of retaining in his adult age the faith they have taught him rests on the conviction that it is God's truth. It is the same with all teaching by human authority. The learner receives what is taught him, because he cannot know the truth immediately by his own faculties. He trusts in the testimony or judgment of others, in respect to those things which he does not know by his own experience or reason, because he believes that their testimony and judgment are certainly or probably exempt, either altogether or to a certain extent, from liability to error; that they cannot in these matters be deceived or deceivers. That is to say, he trusts to them to transmit to him that which God makes known through the natural light of reason. Those whose testimony is entirely credible ought to agree together respecting the same things, and those whose judgments are unerring ought likewise to agree; for truth is one, and contradiction shows that there is error somewhere. If parents, and other instructors who are in the place of parents, could, as such, and by the virtue of their office in the order of nature, give their children and pupils a perfectly true and sufficient instruction, which they might and ought to follow all their lives without fear of error, in respect to religious truth and moral duty, then all parents and instructors should agree in their teaching and precepts; their teaching should be one and catholic. This would have been the case if the human race had remained in the state of original justice and integrity. It is the case now in the Catholic Church, because parents and particular instructors of children and simple people have behind them a catholic and infallible authority. The church teaches through the parents, and the Holy Spirit through the church, and thus all the children of the church are "docibiles Dei"—the docile pupils of God. Adam was to his children a supreme and unerring authority in religion. In like manner Noah was to his children, and Abraham, Isaac, and Jacob to theirs. Moses was the same to the children of Israel, and Jesus Christ is the same in a higher sense, as having authority in his own Person, and being himself Truth and Life—"the Light that enlighteneth every man who cometh into the world."

Every intelligent and reflecting person who professes to be an orthodox believer in Christianity must see and admit, I am very sure, that reason and conscience cannot fully and unconditionally recognize the authority of any teacher in religion who is not supreme and infallible, and must recognize that of one who is. Reason and conscience represent God in the bosom of each individual. An authority which is not supreme and infallible, if it is legitimate, represents God also, but only in the same limited sense that the individual reason and conscience represent him—that is, in so far as it gives satisfactory warrant that its judgments and precepts are in fact exempt from error, and are in conformity to truth and right. As there may be an erroneous conscience and false reasonings in the mind of an individual which need correction; so in the commandments of an authority not supreme, and the judgments of one not infallible, there may be something prescribed as a moral duty or proposed as a religious truth which is sinful or false; and therefore contrary to the precepts and instructions of that supreme authority whose commandments and judgments are capable of being known immediately and directly by the individual conscience and reason; and, if known, must be obeyed, despite all human authority. There is, therefore, no merely temporal authority which is absolutely sovereign, whether in the family or the state. And there is no human spiritual authority which is absolutely sovereign over the reason and conscience, except that which is infallible. It is always supposable that an authority which does not infallibly represent God may require an individual to do that which he knows by his own reason and conscience to be contrary to the law of God, or to profess belief in something which he knows to be contrary to the truth of God; and in either case he has the right and duty of resisting even to death. But once admit that the authority does infallibly represent God, and that reasonable evidence of this is proposed to the reason and conscience, and no possible reason to justify disobedience can be found; because one must disobey his own reason and conscience in disobeying such an authority. This is easily seen by considering the absolute faith and obedience due to Our Lord Jesus Christ in his own person. If we suppose a man, whose wisdom and virtue were the most perfect that a mere man could possibly acquire by all natural means and by the grace of God, to have seen Our Lord while He was living on this earth; we must admit that he would have been obliged to submit his reason and conscience unreservedly to His authority as soon as he knew who He really was. Nevertheless, it would be only the humanity of Christ which was visible to him. He would see his human form, hear his human voice, receive the instruction of his human intellect and the commands of his human will. He would not perceive directly his divine nature, but believe that he was truly God, on his own testimony, by faith. He would be obliged to recognize that as Man his authority was supreme and infallible. He would be obliged to believe every word that he uttered, whatever his previous convictions might have been, and to do whatever he commanded him. To have made an objection that his own reason and conscience did not sanction the doctrine or direction given him by Jesus Christ would have been the most intolerable folly, as well as the most audacious insolence. Now, suppose that Our Lord delegated this supreme and infallible authority to one who should be his representative and vicar on the earth after his own departure, in what respect would the obligation of this man toward the Vicar of Christ differ from his obligation toward Christ himself? Evidently, within the sphere of the delegated authority, in no wise. My Presbyterian friend will admit that the doctrine and law which Jesus Christ commands him to receive are the doctrine and law of Jesus Christ himself, through whatever medium they are transmitted to him with unerring certainty. He will admit that they must be transmitted to him in some way which supplies for the lack of that visible presence of Jesus Christ which his immediate disciples enjoyed. He will admit the necessity of an infallible rule of faith and practice, at least in regard to things necessary to salvation.

But he may still insist that Jesus Christ in his own person is his Infallible Teacher directly through his word contained in the Holy Scripture, which he understands by the light of the Holy Spirit communicated to his own individual spirit. And he may adduce in his own favor the parting promise of Christ: "I will pray the Father, and he shall give you another Comforter, that he may abide with you for ever; even the Spirit of truth; whom the world cannot receive, because it seeth him not, neither knoweth him: but ye know him; for he dwelleth with you, and shall be in you."*

I shall not deny that the Holy Spirit enlightens individual believers to understand and delight in the treasures of the Holy Scripture. This is not, however, the question at issue. The real question is, whether Jesus Christ has left the Scripture, with the light of the Holy Spirit, as the sufficient and only rule of faith to each and every individual believer; and to the church as a mere collection of individuals united together in a common belief, which is constituted by the similitude of their private judgments upon the sense of Holy Scripture.

* St. John xiv. 16, 17.

If this were really the method appointed by Jesus Christ for teaching, propagating, and perpetuating his doctrine and law, it is evident that it would produce unity in faith among the whole multitude of true believers. The Holy Spirit cannot teach diverse doctrines. But diverse doctrines, producing separate sects, have always been found among the multitude of those who profess to be followers of Jesus Christ, and to receive the New Testament as an infallible rule of faith. What is the criterion for determining who are the true disciples of Jesus Christ, truly illuminated by the Holy Spirit? What is the certain test by which each individual can discern the grace of the Holy Spirit in himself from illusions of his own spirit or the spirit of darkness? If it is said that holiness of life is the test, Protestants will find it very difficult to apply this test in such a way as to establish which among their various sects is entitled to claim the possession of the true doctrine. They will find it still more difficult to establish the claim of any form of Protestantism in particular, or of any sort of vague, general system which they may please to call " evangelical," against the ancient or modern Catholic Church. They can bring forward nothing but their own private opinion or sentiment, a mere assertion that such and such doctrines are taught by the Holy Spirit to all true believers, and that those who hold them are the persons whom he really enlightens. But this is of no avail as a certain test and criterion. It is a purely subjective persuasion, in which the subject of it may be easily deluded, and which cannot be the object of a reasonable credibility to any other person, unless it is capable of proof by sound and satisfactory reasons. Therefore Protestants have been forced to throw themselves back upon reason; and to rely upon philosophical, theological, critical, and historical proofs, in order to establish and defend their system of doctrine, and each doctrine of these systems in particular; and to prove that their interpretation of the Holy Scriptures is correct. In the first place, they establish a basis of Natural Theology by rational arguments. They prove the existence, unity, and infinite perfection of God; creation, providence, final causes, the spiritual and immortal essence of the human soul, and the necessity of religion. Upon this basis they establish revealed theology. They adduce the motives of credibility proving the Mosaic and Christian revelation. They proceed to establish the canon of Scripture, its authority and inspiration, and afterwards to investigate its true sense and meaning, and to adduce proofs of one doctrine after another, answering, as well, objections from reason or from different interpretations of revelation. Whatever private revelations or immediate lights of the Holy

Spirit any individual or any number of persons may profess to have received—for example, Montanus, Tertullian, Jacob Böhme, Swedenborg, the Mystics of the fifteenth century, the Chevalier Bunsen, or Edward Irving—they test and judge these by principles of reason and by the sense of the Holy Scripture as received by their own particular sect or theological school. They appeal also to the consent of the multitude of those whom they consider to be the true believers, in holding certain doctrines, and to their inward conviction that the faith by which they believe is produced by the Holy Spirit; but they do not appeal to this as separate from, and independent of, an extrinsic rule of faith. Even in the case of prophets and inspired men, like Moses, Isaias, and St. Paul, they recognize the necessity of an exterior test, an objective evidence, a sanction of some kind, by which obedience to the proclamations they make as messengers of God is made reasonable and obligatory. They do not except Jesus Christ himself; for they establish the reasonableness and the obligation of believing his affirmation that he is the co-equal Son of God the Father, upon evidence, and principally upon prophecy and miracles.

I have no wish to deny the subjective certainty of belief produced directly and immediately by the Holy Spirit in the souls of individuals. Undoubtedly, God can make, and frequently has made, revelations to individual persons, accompanied by such a light that it would be impossible for them to reject them as false or doubtful without a deliberate violence to reason and conscience alike. There have been many other revelations made to individuals which, with greater or less approach to certainty, may be considered, by themselves especially, and by others also who know the reasons of believing them to be divine, as having a claim to credence. Moreover, the Holy Spirit sends his illuminations and inspirations to all men, especially to those who have divine faith; and the faith of a true believer is always a gift of God, and *par excellence* the work of the Holy Spirit. The Holy Spirit is, however, always consistent with himself. He is the Eternal and Unchangeable Truth. All his teachings are consistent with each other. He is the author of the light of reason, and of all revelations, universal and particular. He cannot reveal anything contrary to reason, or reveal to any individual anything contrary to the revelation he has made to all mankind. Where contrary doctrines come into collision, each claiming to proceed from the Holy Spirit, there must be some test or criterion of discernment between them; otherwise certainty is overthrown. In the order of nature reason has the precedence. The light of reason is common and universal, and is the prerequisite condition without which the supernatural light cannot affect the human intellect. It is impossible to believe in God without acknowledging that he created this light. It is by reason that the credibility of revelation is established. It furnishes, moreover, a negative test of the intrinsic credibility of that which claims to be revealed truth. That is, nothing can be received as really revealed by God and to be believed on his veracity which is evidently contrary to reason. And when a public, universal, fully-accredited revelation has been made, it furnishes a test and criterion for trying and judging all private revelations. Nothing which is contrary to any one of its doctrines can be listened to for a moment, as having any claim to credence, or even to examination. Moreover, a private revelation is worthless, unless there is some ground, based on sound reason and on revelation, for giving heed to it. When a sole, sufficient, and unerring rule of faith for Christians has been once established by conclusive proofs, nothing else can be admitted as participating in its authority or independent of it. A Presbyterian, or other Protestant, who regards the Bible as the only, sufficient, and unerring rule of faith, must therefore admit that everything it teaches requires his immediate and unconditional assent as soon as it is discovered to him; and that all private opinions, even if he thinks that he has formed them under the influence of the Holy Spirit, or has received them from persons supposed to be specially enlightened, must give way. He cannot plead that the light of the Holy Spirit within him is of equal authority with the revelation contained in the Scripture, or of any authority at all as distinct from the Scripture itself which is apprehended by this light. The rule is something external, objective, determined, and universal. There is a fixed and objective sense to every paragraph of the Holy Scripture, which the writer intended to express and convey to the reader, and the Holy Spirit intended he should convey. This sense, if ascertainable with certainty or probability, must be ascertained by the application of the ordinary laws of language and the other rules of interpretation, or at least, and even if it is discovered by supernatural light, it must not be in contradiction to them, or overthrow the sense which they establish with certainty.

This was not, indeed, Luther's doctrine. Dr. Dörner, who is perhaps the ablest of modern Lutheran theologians, and thoroughly conversant with Luther's writings, has proved that the author of Protestantism did not recognize any supreme authority in the Holy Scripture. He held that the light of faith is essentially the same with the light of inspiration. The only difference between one person enlightened by the Holy Spirit and any other person likewise enlightened, is in the degree of illumination. Whoever perceives a greater degree of light in another than in himself can receive enlightenment from him; but if he has a greater light in himself, his own light dominates over the lesser light. He had no scruple, therefore, in preferring certain portions of the Scripture to others, correcting some of the utterances of the sacred writers by his own fancied inspiration, judging the Scripture itself by his own subjective convictions, and even rejecting or treating as of dubious value some entire books, as the Epistle of St. James, on his own private authority. Luther was very fond of the writings of the German mystics, especially of one book by an unknown author, called "Theologia Germanica," which has been translated by Miss Winkworth, and published with divers prefatory appendages by Martin Luther, Charles Kingsley, Chevalier Bunsen, and Professor Stowe, that afford a signal evidence of the confusion and contradictions into which Protestants are led by following their own private spirit. Some of the writings of this mystic school are heretical, and others, especially those of Ruysbroeck and Tauler, are strictly orthodox. The utmost that can be said in favor of the "Theologia Germanica" is that it is possible to give an orthodox sense to its ambiguous language. Mystic theology is the most sublime degree of knowledge attainable by man. It is very dangerous, however, unless when controlled by a fixed standard of orthodox doctrine and obedience to authority. The special characteristic of this mystic theology, not in Germany alone, or in the fifteenth century, but everywhere and in all ages, is that it deals with private illuminations and inspirations of the Holy Spirit, and looks at divine truth in an attitude of contemplation and spiritual intuition quite different from the rational investigation and penetration of scholastic theology. Therefore, if the masters and teachers of a spiritual doctrine like this are not thoroughly imbued with a sound philosophical and theological learning, they may easily go astray; even without a wilful intention of departing from orthodox doctrine; or at least express themselves in such an inaccurate and ambiguous manner as to make their writings dangerous; as was the case with Eckhart and the author of "Theologia Germanica." Moreover, restless, self-willed persons, especially if they have a vivid imagination, are liable to run into the greatest illusions and extravagances if they happen to take a fancy to dabble in mysticism. Now, Martin Luther was undoubtedly a genius. His nature was a rich and powerful one. But he was not a philosopher or a theologian. Neither was his moral nature well disciplined and controlled. In the revolution of the sixteenth century he was like what Victor Hugo is now in the revolution of the nineteenth century. The mystic theology had an attraction for his vivid imagination, because it presented before him a vision of a certain elevation of his own individual mind and will which would emancipate him from all authority, and give him a spiritual dominion over others. His own ideas and purposes, exalted into illuminations and inspirations of the Holy Spirit, became, therefore, in his eyes, of divine authority; he was a godlike man, and commissioned to renew and restore the work of Jesus Christ on the earth. As for his theology and system of doctrine, it was no deliberate and consistent scheme, worked out by thought and study, but the result of accident and circumstances. He had but two fixed and essential principles: one was the mystic unification of the individual believer with Christ by faith alone; the other, which was a consequence of the first, the complete independence of the justified man of all external authority over his mind and conscience. These are commonly called justification by faith alone, and the right of private judgment. Both are perversions of mysteries of the faith which are specially brought out in the Catholic mystical theology, viz., the union of the sanctified human soul with Christ, and its interior guidance by the light of the Holy Spirit. And they have sent men wandering away from the doctrine of **Scripture, Tradition, and the Catholic Church** in two different directions. One is the road of Christian or philosophical mysticism. The other is the road of Christian or anti-Christian and anti-Theistic rationalism. Those who retain the idea of union with Christ as God in human nature slide into Christian mysticism and pietism. Those who give up this idea follow private judgment by reasoning on natural principles, and become rationalists, neologists, pantheists, materialists, each one according to his own particular vagary. Germany, where Luther lived, is the homestead and family mansion of all these errors, and from thence they migrate to other lands, destroying everywhere the remnants of Christianity among the children of those who left the church of their fathers in the sixteenth century. The reverence for the authority of the Holy Scriptures, which was formerly so very great in the sects founded by the authors of Protestantism, is at the present time greatly shaken and diminished. It still remains, however, as the strongest breakwater against the rising and rushing stream of infidelity, especially in England, Scotland, and the United States. Among those whose traditional doctrine is Calvinistic the influence of his dogmatic and systematic spirit has been powerfully efficacious in preserving the habit of reverence for what is considered as orthodox belief; and of tenacious adherence to fixed forms of teaching, confessions, creeds, catechisms, standard expositions of doctrine, and other ecclesiastical symbols, in which a common and fixed doctrine is expressed, embodied, and distinctly presented before each individual as the true doctrine contained in Scripture, and obligatory on his conscience; because so clearly revealed by God that he cannot reasonably and conscientiously deny or doubt that it is revealed. The public teachers and preachers of religion are therefore required to conform to this fixed form of doctrine, and their teaching is judged by it. Private persons are also required to conform to it, as a condition of enjoying the privileges of membership in the church. No one is allowed to plead his own individual illumination by the Holy Spirit, or his own private interpretation of the Scripture. On the contrary, he will be told that the Holy Spirit has already made the truth known, and that, if he is really enlightened and inspired by divine grace, he will recognize that truth.

As I am arguing directly only with those who profess to be orthodox Christians in the sense just explained, I am therefore justified in ruling out of count any appeal to private, subjective persuasions of individuals, and taking up singly and solely, **without reference to anything else, the infallible** teaching of Jesus Christ as conveyed to the mind of each one who is capable of receiving it, through the Holy Scriptures.

The argument which I suppose my Presbyterian friend to make is that he has an infallible Teacher, the Lord Jesus Christ himself, who teaches him by his written word, continued in the Old and New Testaments, and that he has therefore no need of any infallible teaching authority in the church. I reply to this that his conclusion is an inference of his own, a mere deduction which has no value except its logical and rational value, and which is therefore to be examined and judged by a merely logical process. So far as the doctrine of the rule of faith is a revealed doctrine, to be believed on the veracity of God, it must be determined, according to my friend's own principles, by the Scripture. In like manner, everything relating to the church, the sacraments, and all doctrines, must be determined by the same rule. All the doctrines of his own sect, and all his own private opinions, must be brought to the same criterion. Whatever, therefore, I have proved or can prove from the Scripture he is bound to receive with an immediate and absolute assent. It avails him nothing to plead that he receives an infallible teaching from Jesus Christ directly through the written word, unless he can prove that this infallible teaching certainly contains in it the whole of his proposition, viz., that the written word is the sole and sufficient rule of faith, to the exclusion of tradition and the authority of the church. And if it can be proved that the Scripture actually teaches the authority of tradition and the church according to the Catholic doctrine, he is forced to admit this by the determination of his own rule of faith. This is not a mere argument *ad hominem*, as it is called—that is, one which merely proves to a man that a certain conclusion follows from his own premises, without necessarily proving that it is really true, because it follows logically from premises which are true. If it were only an argument of this kind, it would merely amount to a proof that one who believes the Bible to be the inspired word of God must believe that the church has supreme, unerring authority in faith, because the Bible teaches this doctrine. It would not, however, by itself, establish the actual truth of the proposition that the Catholic Church possesses this authority. In order that this truth should be established as a revealed truth by an argument from Scripture, it must be proved or admitted as certain that the person to whom this argument is addressed has a sure basis for his belief that the Holy Scripture is really the inspired word of God, or contains the revelation given originally to inspired men and made known by the Son of God in person. Protestants are apt to suppose that a Catholic cannot logically prove the church by the Bible, because, as they say, he must first prove the church before he can appeal to the Bible as the word of God, since it is on the authority of the church that he believes it is the word of God. A Catholic is generally suspected by an evangelical Protestant to whom he proposes Scriptural arguments of not arguing with him in perfect sincerity, but using special pleading; as he is suspected by a rationalist when he adduces arguments from pure reason. But this is wholly a misunderstanding in the case of those who candidly and in good faith cherish this suspicion. These persons of candor and good faith are the only readers with whom I think it worth the pains of arguing, and such readers I am anxious to convince that all my reasoning with them from the Holy Scripture and the orthodox doctrines which they hold, is thoroughly in earnest, and is presented as really based on a solid and certain foundation.

This solid foundation is a well-grounded and reasonable conviction, in the mind and conscience of the persons supposed, that the Bible contains an authentic declaration of revealed truths, and that certain doctrines specified in the beginning of this treatise are among the number of these truths. This conviction may exist, without an explicit knowledge of the infallibility of the church, without a distinct recognition of that authority which really constitutes the true Teaching Church, and, therefore, without any conscious and formal act of the mind perceiving that it receives the faith and the Holy Scripture from the Catholic Church as the medium and instrument of their transmission. The motives of credibility prove sufficiently to convince any rational and upright mind the divine legation of Moses and that of Jesus Christ. The genuineness and authenticity of the books of the Old and New Testaments are also established with certainty. This human and historical faith in Christianity rests on a better and stronger basis than any other common belief which has ever gained a general assent by the effect of moral evidence. Moreover, the doctrines which the founders of the Christian Church taught to their disciples, and which belong to the essence of the pure and original Christianity, can, to a very considerable and important extent, be learned directly from the writings they have left after them, or proved with clearness and certainty from these writings. It is not easy to determine precisely how much of the Catholic faith and doctrine an intelligent and upright heathen could perceive by his natural reason alone to be certainly contained in, and taught by, the Bible, if he should study it diligently. It is enough for me, in arguing with an evangelical Protestant, and especially with a Presbyterian, to state distinctly, as the common ground of discussion between us, that the doctrines assumed as granted by him in the beginning of this treatise, are really taught in, and provable by, the Holy Scripture, which is itself proved by external and internal evidence to be a collection of authentic documents of divine revelation. This is all that is strictly necessary. For it is enough to show that the Jewish religion is correctly represented in the Old Testament, and the Christian religion in the New Testament. Whatever, therefore, is proved by the Old or New Testament to make a part of the religion revealed by God, through Moses, the prophets, Jesus Christ, and the apostles, must be believed as a revealed truth, by force of the motives of credibility which prove the divine legation of Moses and of Jesus Christ. It is, therefore, true that my Presbyterian friend has a human and rational faith in Jesus Christ as an Infallible Teacher. It is also true that he has a certainty of the unerring transmission of the doctrines of this Infallible Teacher through the apostles, and that in some things he can be certain that the apostles have transmitted particular truths, by the text of their writings.

This is enough for what is called the "preamble of faith." That is, it will enable an intelligent and upright person to convince himself very easily that the apostles in the name of Christ established the Catholic Church, and left in it their own supreme authority to the end of time; and he will then receive with docile humility the entire faith from the church, as the proximate rule of faith. Among other articles of faith he will receive this one: that the Holy Scripture, composed of a specified number of books, is the word of God,. written by the inspiration of the Holy Spirit. This is a quite different proposition from the one which precedes. By the preceding proposition, it is historically and rationally certain that the writings of the apostles are authentic documents of the religion they were commissioned to establish, and that they contain, among other things, evidence of their having established a certain ecclesiastical authority to last until the end of time. By the second proposition, it is a revealed truth that such and such books constitute a sacred canon of Scripture, which was written by the inspiration of the Holy Spirit, and is the word of God. I will here cite the definition of inspiration given by Dr. Murray, professor of dogmatic theology in the Royal College of Maynooth, in his admirable Treatise on the Church. "I adopt the definition of inspiration given by Marchini, and approved and sanctioned by Perrone, as in respect to its substance altogether certain, viz., ' That special impulse of the Holy Spirit moving the person to write, with a direction and presence governing his mind and spirit while writing, which does not permit him to err, and causes him to write those things which God wills.' Therefore, that any Scripture be inspired, it is requisite: (1) That the writer be excited to write by the Holy Spirit; (2) that in writing he be not only kept exempt from all error whatsoever; but also (3), although inspiration is not requisite to give him knowledge of things which he already knows, since, by the very supposition, they are already known, there is requisite a positive action on the mind of the writer, in respect both to those things which are already known, and those not before known, to make him write them, so far as their substance is concerned, and in the act of writing; (4) what, in fact, is included in the foregoing, that only those things which God wills should be written, all other matters being excluded."* The more orthodox Protestants have generally held this doctrine of plenary inspiration, and still hold it. I have all along taken this doctrine as granted by those I am specially addressing, and I have, therefore, constantly cited the declarations of Holy Scripture as not merely trustworthy or even certainly unerring statements of that which God has revealed, but as themselves the very word of God. Now, before I conclude this treatise, I

* "De Eccl.," Vol. II., disp. xi. sect. i. § 22.

shall furnish evidence that the doctrine thus assumed as a divine truth, and admitted by those whom I address, is really true because it is taught by the church, and this evidence will therefore have a retroactive effect upon the whole argument. Nevertheless, I do not wish to content myself with this, but to show also what is the real and determining motive of credibility which has preserved such a deeply-rooted and general conviction among Protestants, that the Scripture is, strictly speaking, and in the Catholic sense, the inspired word of God.

In the first place, it is certainly not any frequent and distinct statements found in the Scriptures themselves. They do not contain any clear and explicit rules for determining the canon, or explain the specific difference of a canonical book which distinguishes it from a book which contains sound and wholesome doctrine or true and edifying history, though it is not canonical. There are some passages which imply the doctrine of plenary inspiration, if that doctrine is already proved to be the common belief at the time these passages were written. There are also allusions in some canonical books to others, as belonging to the Scripture. This scanty and indirect proof is not, however, sufficient to settle precisely the exact canon, or to determine clearly, much less to make known at first hand, to an ordinary reader, the nature and extent of the inspiration of that which is Holy Scripture as such.

Let my Presbyterian friend ask himself why he believed at the age of six or nine years with such an undoubting assent that his Bible contained the whole of inspired scripture, and nothing but inspired scripture, truly inspired in such a sense that God is its author. I have no doubt for myself that in every case a child who is taught this believes it simply because he is taught it by his parents and religious instructors. If he becomes familiar with the Bible by frequently hearing it read and by reading it, this belief is confirmed and strengthened by the internal evidence which the sacred books give of themselves. When the child grows up, and acquires a more extended and explicit knowledge of the grounds of his religious belief, what is it which convinces his mind that the books he was taught to regard as the inspired word of God are certainly genuine, authentic, and inspired? And if he is called upon to vindicate and prove his belief, what argument will he adduce as the most conclusive? In a general way, undoubtedly, the internal evidence of the divine origin and nature of the religion revealed through Moses and Jesus Christ, and of the genuine, authentic character of the documents of that religion, will convince him, and enable him to vindicate his convictions. But for a precise, categorical proof that the canon contains such and such books he will be forced to recur to the authority of a universal and primitive tradition. These books, and no others, he will say, belong to the canon of the New Testament, because the testimony of all competent witnesses, everywhere and always, proves that they, and they alone, had the original sanction of the apostles. In regard to the Old Testament, he will say the same thing. And he will justly consider the concurrence of the Jews with all Christians in respect to the Hebrew Scriptures as an additional and irrefragable proof of their authenticity. His ignorance of the grounds on which the canonicity of the Hellenistic books of the Old Testament rests does not invalidate the soundness of his judgment respecting those which are in the Hebrew canon.

In regard to inspiration, it is the same thing. He knows that the founders of the Protestant sects received their doctrine of inspiration from the Catholic Church; that the Eastern Christians hold the same doctrine; and that it is the orthodox tradition of the synagogue received from the old time before the coming of Christ. In a word, he virtually recognizes the church, as established by Moses, and reconstituted in its universal form by the apostles, as the guardian and keeper of the Holy

Scripture, and the witness to its integrity and inspiration, in this respect indefectible and preserved from error by the special providence of God.

So far, then, he never finds any good reason for rejecting or doubting the instruction of his parents and religious teachers, which is really the instruction of the universal church reaching him through the medium of their testimony. Although he does not know that the church is infallible, yet he is reasonably convinced that, in this respect, the testimony of that whole body of Christians, within whose limits the true church must be somewhere found does not and cannot deceive him. He has, therefore, the revelation of God sufficiently proposed to him in the Holy Scriptures, as the Written Word, inspired by the Holy Ghost, and of course infallible, in so far as the true sense of the Scripture is manifest on the face of it, or capable of being determined with certainty by the means at his command.

Let us see, now, what value there is in his presumption that his own sect is the true church, or a part of it, and really holds the essential doctrine of Christ, and lawfully administers the sacraments, because it is the channel through which the Holy Scripture and certain doctrines manifestly pertaining to the Christian faith have been transmitted to him. That he must begin with this presumption, and is justified in following the teaching he has received until he finds a grave reason for doubting it, is manifest. But a presumption of this kind can never shut out the right and obligation of paying due attention to such a doubt, and of rejecting all that part of the instruction one has received from the sect of which he is a disciple, as soon as he has a sufficient reason for doing so.

This presumption is very much weakened as soon as he knows that his sect differs, in regard to those things which belong to the very essence of the church, of Christian doctrine, and of the sacraments, from the great majority of professing Christians who receive the Holy Scripture as the inspired word of God. Why should he presume that his sect is right, to the exclusion of other Protestant sects? If he says that it is not exclusively right, but that the pure church is composed of all these sects together, why should he presume that they are right in contradistinction to the Catholic and the Eastern Churches? It is not safe to act on a presumption that the sense of the Holy Scripture is rightly understood by a certain number of individuals professing to follow private and individual illumination from the Holy Spirit, when a much larger number, in the present and during many foregoing ages, hold a different or contrary sense. Something more certain and decisive is necessary, that he may discern where the right is to be ascertained with security to his conscience. For the present he is thrown back upon himself, and obliged to make use of his own reason and judgment, with what light he can obtain from God by prayer. He must examine the pretence of his own church to teach him the truth, and to give him the sacraments. As soon as he begins to do this seriously, this pretence will be found to have no warrant whatever. It is in contradiction with itself. For, on the one hand, as we have seen, and as a very little reflection will show to any one, the doctrine which he has learned has been given him by instruction, and by practically following the Catholic method of teaching by authority a certain sense of the Scripture which is positively determined, and by which the text of the same is interpreted and understood. On the other, this sense is distinctly affirmed to be nothing more than the result of the agreement of a number of persons in their own private judgment of the meaning of Scripture, founded on their own personal examination, and deriving its value from the illumination which each one separately has received from the Holy Spirit. Each one is referred to the Scripture, that he may receive the truth directly and immediately from the inspired word of God. The Presbyterian Church and the other sects existing among the disciples of Luther and Calvin thus in the same breath claim and disclaim authority to teach, and betray in their uncertain, inconsistent speech their utter want of any legitimate possession of right to teach, as a person of unsettled mind betrays his insanity by his incoherent conversation.

The serious Protestant enquirer may also very easily perceive, from all the foregoing considerations presented to him in this book, that the certain, indisputable truths of divine revelation which he has learned through his teachers are just those which they have merely transmitted to him from the ancient and universal tradition. Of themselves, they give him nothing except the denial of all exterior authority, and a mass of disputes in which they have been engaged, after the manner of the rival factions of Louisiana and Arkansas, and which on their principles can never be settled. What is to be done in such a case? For the present the serious enquirer must continue to enquire and search until he finds the true church. His own sect and all the sects of the reformation of Luther refer him to the Scriptures. All churches that can possibly claim his attention recognize their authority and appeal to it in support and proof of their own right. Let him examine, then, with due rectitude of mind, humility of heart, piety of intention, and diligence of search, what the Scriptures teach in such a way that he can be sure of their true sense. The Lord said to the Jews on one occasion: "Search the Scriptures; for in them ye think ye have eternal life, and they are they which testify of me." Certainly, the true church may say the same to all who believe the Bible to be the inspired word of God. And, in point of fact, all that previous searching which I suppose my reader to have made, and that which he has made while reading this book, must have brought him already very near to the discovery of the true church. For not only have I shown that the presumption in favor of any one or any collection among Protestant sects being the church or any part of it, is without anything to sustain it objectively, but I have proved that these sects, so far as they follow Lutheran or Calvinistic doctrine, subvert and deny several doctrines of faith, and are therefore heretical. Moreover, the whole course of this argument has at least shown that there is a violent presumption in favor of the Catholic Church.

I will now proceed to prove directly from the Scripture that there is and can be but one church, which is the Catholic Church, founded by Jesus Christ, and existing in unbroken continuity to the end of time, as the only Way of Salvation for mankind.

CHAPTER SIXTH.

The Nature, Attributes, and Organic Principles of the True Church proved from Scripture—Proof that the Holy, Catholic, Apostolic, Roman Church is the One True Church founded by Jesus Christ—The Only Way of Salvation is in the Catholic Church—Conclusion.

THE proposition to be proved in this chapter includes two distinct parts: First, The Scripture teaches that there is and can be but one church, founded by Jesus Christ, and existing in unbroken continuity to the end of time, as the only Way of Salvation for all mankind. Second, the Scripture teaches that the Catholic Church, or that society which in its universal extension through time and space exists in organic unity under the monarchy of St. Peter and his successors, is the one true church founded by Jesus Christ.

It is not necessary to prove the admitted fact that Jesus Christ founded a visible church. What must be proved is that he founded it in organic unity and perpetual organic continuity, as the only Way of Salvation, and therefore containing in itself all the means of grace which conduce to salvation. That the Son of God, before his incarnation, founded the Jewish Church in organic unity and a limited perpetuity—that is, to last until he came on the earth in human form—is undoubted. It is therefore to be presumed that he founded the Christian Church in organic unity and in a perpetuity without limits, except those which bound time itself. This presumption cannot be set aside, except by showing that a church without perpetual organic unity would be more perfect. I have shown, however, in a former part of this volume, that this cannot be true; wherefore the presumption stands, and is really an amply sufficient proof of the thesis. I will add to it, however, not by any means the whole positive proof, from express statements of Scripture, but a sufficient quantity of it, premising that this presumption must rule the interpretation of texts, and determine their sense in favor of organic, visible unity, when they are otherwise capable, or may be thought capable, of another sense.

The unity of organization and consequently of government in the church is proved, in the first place, from the names and titles given to it everywhere throughout the Scripture.* One of these names is " body," clearly denoting the corporate unity of the church. Robinson defines the Greek word used in the New Testament in the passages referred to as signifying in its primary sense

---

* The author acknowledges his great obligation to Dr. Murray (" De Ecclesià ") for the materials of this part of the present treatise.

"an organized whole made up of parts and members." As Cornelius à Lapide (on Rom. xii. 4) well remarks: "As in a body there are four properties; first, corporeal unity; second, diversity of members; third, diversity of functions in the single members; fourth, aptitude and power in each member for fulfilling its function; so there is a precise resemblance of all these things in the church and in its individual members, to wit, the Christian faithful." The church is, therefore, a corporation, which Webster defines to be "a body politic or corporate, formed and authorized by law to act as a single individual."

Another still more specific and significant name is "kingdom." The Jews understood this in a literal sense. Whatever was false in their conception Our Lord repeatedly and explicitly corrected. We must, therefore, take their sense as correct in all respects besides that one which he condemned. Now, their error consisted altogether in the purely temporal and political nature which they ascribed to the kingdom of the Messias, with the consequences following from this erroneous conception. We must therefore regard the kingdom of Jesus Christ as really and truly a monarchy, a visible society of men bound together by laws and government; though a spiritual monarchy, having a supernatural end, distinct from civil society and superior to it, according to the Catholic idea of the church.

The other metaphorical names, "city," "house," "temple," "sheepfold," "mustard-seed" growing up to a great tree with wide branches, denote unity in a similar manner. But especially the holy and tender names of "spouse" and "bride" given to the church show that she is one and alone, and indissolubly bound in sacramental union to Christ, all others who claim the name being necessarily vile impostors. "One is my dove, my perfect one." *

The context of the particular passages in which these names of the church occur amplifies and illustrates the idea of unity in a manner which only a separate treatise could exhibit with due clearness and completeness. Let any one read the prophets with this intention in view, and he will be overawed by their incomparable splendor of language and imagery in describing the kingdom of God on earth, the church of the Messias whose reign they foretold.

"Arise, shine; for thy light is come, and the glory of the Lord is risen upon thee. For, behold, darkness shall cover the earth, and gross darkness the people: but the Lord shall arise upon thee, and his glory shall be seen upon thee. And the Gentiles shall come to thy light, and kings to the brightness of thy rising. Lift up thine eyes

* Cant. v. 8.

round about, and see: all they gather themselves together, they come to thee: thy sons shall come from far, and thy daughters shall be nursed at thy side. Then thou shalt see, and flow together, and thine heart shall fear, and be enlarged; because the abundance of the sea shall be converted unto thee, the forces of the Gentiles shall come unto thee. The multitude of camels shall cover thee, the dromedaries of Midian and Ephah; all they from Sheba shall come: they shall bring gold and incense; and they shall shew forth the praises of the Lord. All the flocks of Kedar shall be gathered together unto thee, the rams of Nebaioth shall minister unto thee: they shall come up with acceptance on mine altar, and I will glorify the house of my glory. Who are these that fly as a cloud, and as the doves to their windows? Surely the isles shall wait for me, and the ships of Tarshish first, to bring thy sons from far, their silver and their gold with them, unto the name of the Lord thy God, and to the Holy One of Israel, because he hath glorified thee. And the sons of strangers shall build up thy walls, and their kings shall minister unto thee: for in my wrath I smote thee, but in my favor have I had mercy on thee. Therefore thy gates shall be open continually; they shall not be shut day nor night; that men may bring unto thee the forces of the Gentiles, and that their kings may be brought. For the nation and kingdom that will not serve thee shall perish; yea, those nations shall be utterly wasted. The glory of Lebanon shall come unto thee, the fir tree, the pine tree, and the box together, to beautify the place of my sanctuary; and I will make the place of my feet glorious. The sons also of them that afflicted thee shall come bending unto thee; and all they that despised thee shall bow themselves down at the soles of thy feet; and they shall call thee, The city of the Lord, The Zion of the Holy One of Israel. Whereas thou hast been forsaken and hated, so that no man went through thee, I will make thee an eternal excellency, a joy of many generations. Thou shalt also suck the milk of the Gentiles, and shalt suck the breast of kings: and thou shalt know that I the Lord am thy Saviour and thy Redeemer, the mighty One of Jacob. For brass I will bring gold, and for iron I will bring silver, and for wood brass, and for stones iron: I will also make thy officers peace, and thine exactors righteousness. Violence shall no more be heard in thy land, wasting nor destruction within thy borders; but thou shalt call thy walls Salvation, and thy gates Praise. The sun shall be no more thy light by day; neither for brightness shall the moon give light unto thee: but the Lord shall be unto thee an everlasting light, and thy God thy glory. Thy sun shall no more go down; neither shall thy moon withdraw itself: for the Lord shall be thine everlasting light, and the days of thy mourning shall be ended. Thy people also shall be all righteous: they shall inherit the land for ever, the branch of my planting, the work of my hands, that I may be glorified. A little one shall become a thousand, and a small one a strong nation: I the Lord will hasten it in his time." *

This one passage must suffice as a specimen of the prophecies concerning the church. The apostles express the same ideas in a calmer and more didactic form in many parts of their epistles. For instance, St. Paul, writing to the Ephesians, declares that God raised Jesus from the dead, "and set him at his own right hand in the heavenly places, far above all principality, and power, and might, and dominion, and every name that is named, not only in this world, but also in that which is to come: and hath put all things under his feet, and gave him to be the head over all things to the church, *which is his body, the fulness of him that filleth all in all.*" And again: "Ye are no more strangers and foreigners, but fellow-citizens with the saints, and of the household of God; and are built upon the foundation of the apostles and prophets, Jesus Christ himself being the chief corner-stone; in whom all the building fitly framed together groweth unto a holy temple in the Lord."†

* Is. c. lx.   † Eph. i. 20–23; ii. 19–21.

Our Lord himself declares that "there shall be **one** fold and one shepherd"; and he prayed with an efficacious prayer, which no failure on the part of man could prevent from being fulfilled, that the apostles and their disciples for ever might be joined in a unity similar to that of the Three Divine Persons, which should give the church a glory like his own, and be a manifest sign to all men of the reality of his divine mission. "That they all may be one, as thou, Father, art in me, and I in thee, that they also may be one in us: that the world may believe that thou hast sent me. And the glory which thou gavest me, I have given them; that they may be one, even as we are one."*

That there is and can be but one true church is further proved by the denunciation of heresy, schism, sects, and sectarian teachers in the New Testament. "A man that is a heretic, after the first and second admonition, reject; knowing that he that is such is subverted, and sinneth, being condemned of himself." "But there were false prophets also among the people, even as there shall be false teachers among you, who privily shall bring in damnable heresies, even denying the Lord that bought them, and bring upon themselves swift destruction." "For such are false apostles, deceitful **workers**, transforming themselves into the apostles

---

* St. John x. 16; xvii. 21, 22.

of Christ. And no marvel; for Satan himself is transformed into an angel of light. Therefore it is no great thing if his ministers also be transformed as the ministers of righteousness; whose end shall be according to their works."*

It is evident that the faithful formed one communion during the apostolic age, and that those who set themselves up as rivals to the apostles and to the clergy of the apostolic communion, teaching a different doctrine and making separate sects, were denounced as impostors and ministers of Satan, who led their followers to destruction, and not to salvation. And this leads me to the consideration of the hierarchical constitution which Jesus Christ gave to his church, and which was the law of its external and visible unity.

It is scarcely necessary to go over again the oft-repeated argument of the apostolic commission given by Our Lord to St. Peter and his associates. It is plainly written in the Holy Scripture, where it can be known and read of all men. No one of those who have read and sincerely revere the New Testament will deny that the apostles were universal governors and teachers of the church, and that the one plain mark of the true church, in which the pure word of God was preached, and the sacraments rightly administered according to Christ's ordinance,

* Tit. iii. 10; 2 St. Peter ii. 1; 2 Cor. xi. 13–15.

was, during the apostolic age, its submission to apostolic rule and doctrine. St. John declares this in express words: "We are of God: he that knoweth God heareth us; he that is not of God heareth not us. *Hereby know we the spirit of truth, and the spirit of error.*"* The point which I wish to insist on is that, by this apostolic commission, a permanent hierarchical order was established, an *Ecclesia Docens*, a Teaching Church, supreme and therefore infallible as a proximate Rule of Faith, with the other consequent and necessary powers of making and enforcing laws, under whose obedience the only way of salvation can alone be found. These two essential principles of the constitution of the church are most closely connected with, and involved in, each other. A hierarchical order to which the office of teaching and law-giving is committed by divine authority, without any restriction or appeal and which the faithful are bound unreservedly to obey, must be secured from error so far as to prevent its vitiating the doctrine and law of which it is the authorized expositor and executive magistracy. Under a dispensation like that of the universal church, this security requires that it should be made infallible in faith and morals. A permanent and universal hierarchy cannot subsist without infallibility. The converse of this is also true. An in-

---

* 1 St. John iv. 6.

fallible authority cannot subsist in the church without a hierarchical order. All the proofs from the Scripture, therefore, for the one, are also proofs of the other. These proofs are both clear and abundant.

The Old Testament furnishes some which are most striking. The prophet Isaias, describing the Christian church, says: "A highway shall be there, and a way, and it shall be called The way of holiness; the unclean shall not pass over it; but it shall be for those: (it shall be for you a direct way—*Vulgate*), the wayfaring men, though fools, shall not err therein." Again: "O thou afflicted, tossed with tempest, and not comforted, behold, I will lay thy stones with fair colors, and lay thy foundations with sapphires. And I will make thy windows of agates, and thy gates of carbuncles, and all thy borders of pleasant stones. And all thy children shall be taught of the Lord; and great shall be the peace of thy children. . . . No weapon that is formed against thee shall prosper; and every tongue that shall rise against thee thou shalt condemn."* That which the prophet sets forth with such splendor of imagery St. Paul declares in plain, set terms, which, though brief, are perfectly distinct and precise: "These things write I unto thee, hoping to come unto thee shortly: but if I tarry long, that thou

* Is. xxxv., liv.

mayest know how thou oughtest to behave thyself in the house of God, which is the church of the living God, *the pillar and ground of the truth.*" * The church is the royal and secure way of salvation, teaching that faith and commanding those works by which men must be saved, until the end of the world. Therefore she has been established in a perpetual order and an infallible permanence in faith, as the necessary means of her indefectibility, by the institution of her Founder. The instructions by virtue of which the apostles were empowered to lay the foundations of the indestructible edifice of the church were given to them, specifically and minutely, by Our Lord, during the great forty days which elapsed between Easter Sunday and the Ascension: " being seen of them forty days, and speaking of the things pertaining to the kingdom of God." † Extraordinary gifts of the Holy Spirit were also infused into them on the Day of Pentecost, by virtue of which they were enabled to remember and understand unerringly the verbal instructions received from the Lord, and were directed in respect to all things requisite to the solid foundation of the church. The constitution which they gave to the church is the one which is by its very nature perpetual and unalterable. It is a most violent and gratuitous assumption, and one contrary

* 1 Tim. iii. 14, 15.   † Acts i. 3.

to all probability, that Our Lord should have established a provisional and temporary constitution, hierarchy, government, rule of faith, in the very beginning of the universal church, to be succeeded afterwards by institutions totally different. Those who make it are bound to give explicit and clear proof from the canonical scriptures of the New Testament to justify their hypothesis, which they ever have and ever must fail to do. I have proved that the church which Christ founded was One; it was necessarily Catholic as soon as it was opened to the Gentiles and they began to flock into its precincts; no one will question that it was Holy and Apostolic. Because it was first established with these four marks, it must continue to bear them to the end of time. Apostolic in constitution and government during its first epoch, that is, hierarchical, with a subordination of its parts and members to a supreme, infallible teaching and ruling authority; apostolic, hierarchical, subject to sovereign authority and jurisdiction over the mind and conscience of individual members, in respect to faith and morals, it must continue, to the end of the world. Whatever relates solely to the first foundation and institution of the church, its perpetual laws, its sacraments, and other things of like nature, which need to be done and can be done but once for all, must, indeed, be regarded as a special, extraordinary, and transient attribute of the apostolic office. But all that relates to the exercise of powers and functions which in their nature are continuous and perpetual must be permanent, and the office itself must be as permanent as the end for which it was established. The divine revelation once completed, there is no further occasion for the gift of inspiration. The essential order of the church, and the sacraments, once established, the power given to this end ceases of itself. The gifts of miracles, of speaking all languages, of prophecy, etc., their end being accomplished, cease to be the regular and invariable adjuncts of the apostolic character. There are certain powers which the first founders and authors of a divine society must have *as founders*, and first in the line of rulers, and which cannot be transmitted to their successors even as attributes of supreme and sovereign power. The power of teaching and ruling is one, however, in its nature continuous and permanent. A hierarchical jurisdiction, so ordered as to bind all the members of the body into one corporate organization under one supreme authority, is of the very essence of a church which has visible unity and catholicity in all parts of the world, through all time. This is evident in itself. But it is also explicitly and clearly declared in the New Testament. Not only is the grant of authority to the apostles for founding the church expressly stated, but the perpetuity of their office in a line of apostolic succession is just as expressly and distinctly declared, as many learned and able authors have repeatedly proved at great length and by the most unanswerable arguments, and as all Christians, except a very small minority, have always and everywhere believed. There is no need to repeat these arguments here. The words of the Holy Scripture are familiar to all who read it. They are few, but they are clear and emphatic. They tell us that Our Lord commanded the apostles to preach the Gospel in all the world and to all men; to teach them the observance of all the commandments they had received from him; to baptize them into the communion of the church; to bear the keys of the kingdom of heaven; to remit and retain sins; and that he promised to be with them always, to the end of the world. Moreover, he likened their mission from himself to his own mission from the Father, and declared that to receive or reject, to hear or despise them, would be equivalent to paying honor or manifesting contempt toward his own royal and divine Person. It is evident, therefore, that the individual apostles personally commissioned by Our Lord were not endowed with a power merely personal, destined to expire with them, but with one destined to survive in a hierarchical order deriving its authority from them by lawful succession to the end of the world.

Moreover, Our Lord made a specific and distinct promise to send the Holy Spirit to teach the apostles and their successors, to keep them in the truth, and to enable them to fulfil their office as teachers of all mankind to the end of the world. "I will pray the Father, and he shall give you another Comforter, that he may *abide with you for ever;* even the Spirit of truth; whom the world cannot receive, because it seeth him not, neither knoweth him: but ye know him; for he dwelleth with you, and shall be in you. . . . The Comforter, which is the Holy Ghost, whom the Father will send in my name, he shall teach you all things, and bring all things to your remembrance, whatsoever I have said unto you."*

The pretence of sectarians to the illumination of the Holy Spirit and the possession of the truth, and all the illusions of false mysticism, of private, interior light, of private judgment on the Scripture, of immediate union with Christ apart from the communion of the true church—the whole baseless, shadowy fabric of Luther and Calvin is swept away by these declarations of Scripture when correctly explained and understood according to the ancient tradition and doctrine of Catholic antiquity. It is

---

* St. John xiv. 16, 17, 26.

to the church, and eminently to the teaching church, the apostolic hierarchy, deriving its authority and doctrine from the apostles, that the Holy Spirit is promised and given, as a perpetual gift for all ages. From the hands of this apostolic hierarchy the canonical Scriptures are received, stamped with a divine sanction as inspired writings, guarded, preserved, and authenticated, with their true sense and exposition, and with the apostolic tradition which is a supplementary and concurrent rule of faith. The teaching of the apostolic hierarchy, derived from Scripture and Tradition, and, by the perpetual assistance of the Holy Spirit, unerring and infallible, is the proximate and immediate rule of faith to all the children of God in Christ.

What the true church, founded by Jesus Christ, was, is therefore plain from the Holy Scripture. Where it was, and which society is identical with the original apostolic communion, is also manifest from the New Testament. The Churches of Rome, Alexandria, Antioch, Jerusalem, Ephesus, Corinth, Smyrna, Crete, governed by the apostles themselves and by St. Mark, St. Timothy, St. Titus, St. Ignatius, St. Polycarp, and the other bishops established by the apostles or their associates and successors; the churches warned, saluted, and shown in prophetic vision by St. John the future which was before them—these churches, bound together in one universal church, are the church of the New Testament. They make up the catholic church of the primitive period, which appears indistinctly in the scanty records of the ante-Nicene writers, and bursts forth in glory at the Council of Nice, when the sword of Constantine is seen glittering above that august assembly to protect the faith proclaimed by their decree. This is the "One, Holy, Catholic, and Apostolic Church" of the Nicene Creed.

I have reserved what is by far the clearest, strongest, and most conclusive proof from the New Testament of the organic unity, hierarchical constitution, sovereign and infallible authority, perpetual, unchangeable continuity, of the true, Catholic Church of Jesus Christ, until the last.

It has been already sufficiently proved that the church was constituted in organic unity as a body politic and a visible kingdom. It has also been proved that a hierarchy, or sacred order of spiritual rulers and judges, beginning with the apostles, was established, which should be perpetual and indefectible. This true, catholic church has been identified with that grand, organized multitude of Christian prelates, clergy, and people which existed in historical continuity from the apostolic age to the conversion of Constantine, and was represented in the Œcumenical Council of Nice. Not only all communions possessing or pretending to an episcopal succession in unbroken descent from the apostles, but all others, called orthodox, recognize and acknowledge this church of the first three centuries as the Catholic Church, in contradistinction from all other sects then existing. Its episcopal constitution, admitted as an undoubted historical fact in respect to the period of the Nicene Council, is not, indeed, admitted by Protestants generally as of apostolic institution. I have not dwelt at length on the proof from the New Testament of the divine institution and special powers of the order of bishops in the church; because I have a more direct and conclusive line of argument before me, proving the essentially episcopal constitution of distinct and local churches as involved in the essentially papal constitution of the church catholic. I have proved enough, however, in a general way, to make it evident that hierarchy and subordination must have been established in the order of the clergy, and a supreme power, like that which the apostles exercised, controlling the rulers and teachers of particular portions of the flock, and keeping them in unity of doctrine and discipline. I proceed now to prove that the organic unity of the hierarchy and the church was constituted in a monarchical regimen, or a sovereign authority delegated to one supreme bishop, the Ruler,

Teacher and Judge of the whole Catholic Church.

The very idea of the church, as one body politic, extending over the whole world, demands this monarchical regimen as the only constitution morally sufficient and possible, except by a constantly miraculous providence. The notion of independent congregations, each one governing itself, destroys the very conception of universal, corporate unity. Corporate unity may exist in this way in small bodies. But each one of them makes a separate unit by itself. Independent dioceses, provinces, or patriarchates likewise make separate though larger units. Councils or courts composed of prelates, or of representatives appointed in some fixed manner, executing a supreme power, may to a certain extent preserve a corporate unity within tolerably large limits. This will be very precarious, however, unless there is at least some presiding and administrative head. Mere Presbyterian or Episcopal government is at best only fit to sustain national churches. It is wholly unfit and inadequate for the preservation of unity in the church catholic. The church catholic, as a body, must have one head, as a kingdom must have a sovereign. The hierarchical system, however well organized, with its metropolitans, primates, and patriarchs, is an arch without its keystone. It is liable to the disaster of separation, schism, divergence in doctrine and discipline, mutual hostility among its constituent parts. As it is necessary that there should be pastors for the distinct flocks of the fold of Christ, and chief pastors over these, so there must be one supreme pastor over the whole fold, all the shepherds and all the sheep. There must be a power to govern bishops, to judge them, to punish them, as well as a power to rule over priests and people. No matter how far the gradation of ranks among bishops is carried; if you subordinate suffragans to metropolitans, metropolitans to primates, and all primates to three or four patriarchs, the patriarchs themselves must have a Supreme Bishop over them to govern them, judge them, and, if necessary, to punish them.

It is a mere evasion to pretend that the church requires no visible, earthly head, because Our Lord Jesus Christ is its head, its king, and its high-priest. He is the head, the ruler, the pastor, the priest of every diocese and parish. He is the teacher of every individual. He is the Word of God. God is the Father of every baptized child. One might as well say, then, that we need no pastors, no teachers, no Bible, no parents; as to say that the kingdom of Christ needs no earthly sovereign. Our Lord is a king who is invisible and inaccessible to men on the earth in the ordinary and human way. Therefore he cannot personally exercise his office as sovereign in an ordinary and human way. He can only exercise it by a vicegerent, as an emperor governs a distant and dependent kingdom. The royalty of Jesus Christ as sovereign in the spiritual order, combining the offices of prophet, priest, and king in one monarchical supremacy over the church militant on earth, requires that he should have a representative, the head of the hierarchy, from whom all inferior prelates derive their authority, and who rules over all the faithful through them, uniting all in one through his own supremacy. The prophet Zacharias pointed out Joshua, which in Greek is Jesus, the son of Josedech the high-priest, as a type of this sacerdotal royalty. "Then take silver and gold, and make crowns, and set them upon the head of Joshua the son of Josedech, the high-priest; and speak unto him, saying, Thus speaketh the Lord of hosts, saying, Behold the man whose name is The BRANCH; and he shall grow up out of his place, and he shall build the temple of the Lord: Even he shall build the temple of the Lord; and he shall bear the glory, and shall sit and rule upon his throne; and he shall be a priest upon his throne. . . . And the Lord shall be King over all the earth: in that day shall there be one Lord, and his name One."*

This prophecy most clearly designates the tem-

* Zach. vi. 11-13, xiv. 9.

poral reign of Our Lord Jesus Christ over the Catholic Church, his earthly kingdom. Invisibly, he reigns over it from his throne in the heavens, at the right hand of the Father. Visibly, he reigns by his vicegerent, a visible priest upon a visible throne, ruling in the name and by the authority of Christ, as his earthly Vicar. To this sublime position he raised St. Peter, to whom he communicated plenary powers, to be transmitted to his successors until the end of time. "And I say also unto thee, that thou art Peter (Rock), and upon this rock I will build my church." The church is a kingdom, that is, a state essentially constituted upon the monarchical principle. The monarchy of its rightful, perpetual, divinely-appointed royal line is therefore its foundation. The monarchical right and power given to St. Peter occupy in the spiritual edifice of the Catholic Church the same position which the foundation has in a material building. The foundation sustains, and, as it were, *rules* the whole edifice —*i.e.*, by its underlying strength, solidity, and support, it keeps the whole building in order and every portion of it in its proper place, thus making it firm and durable, preventing its sinking and toppling over, and thus losing its structural form in a mass of fragments. The foundation of a building is the principle of its unity, repose, order, and durability. The Rock on which the church is built is that which bears the same relation to the unity, order, and stability of the church during the whole period of its existence and throughout its entire extent. It is called a rock because that is the most solid and immovable kind of foundation for a building, and therefore fitly represents the unchangeable and immovable strength of the spiritual monarchy established in Peter and his successors by Our Lord. This monarchy must last, therefore, and be the support of the whole church, until the end of time. It is more solid and durable than even the church itself which is indestructible, because it is the basis of the indestructible durability of the church. It is so in its own nature, and by virtue of the admirable constitution of its powers as a central, spiritual sovereignty surrounded by a numerous, well-organized hierarchy and a vast Christendom, whose political order is subordinated to it, and forms its impregnable bulwark. Its natural durability would not be sufficient, however, without a superadded supernatural strength and a special providence of God to preserve it from being subverted and overthrown. The name given to the founder of this spiritual monarchy, Peter, was given to him to denote that his strength was received from Christ, and that the foundation of the church in the See of Peter was made like a base of rock by an act of his divine power. His special, perpetual providence is promised and pledged to it, unconditionally and in perpetuity, to preserve it, and by it to preserve the church, until the end of the world. "And the gates of hell shall not prevail against it." This is a positive promise of unbroken, historical continuity to that very same organized, visible society of which St. Peter was the head, to the end of time. Therefore it could never cease to be the true church, and be succeeded by a new one, or a re-formed and reconstructed one. It is a promise of indefectibility in faith and morals, which requires and involves not only a passive but an active inerrancy and infallibility. It is a promise of perpetuity in unity of organization, by the continued supremacy of the successors of Peter over the church, and the subjection of the hierarchy and faithful of the catholic church to their authority; a promise of victory over false religion, heresy, schism, infidelity, sin, and all wicked assaults of civil potentates, demagogues, or revolutionary parties. All these are gates of hell. Against these gates the church, and the foundation of the church; the catholic multitude of pastors and faithful, and the papacy; are made for ever impregnable by the almighty word of Christ. The principle of the unity and invincibility of the church is the supremacy of the successors of Peter. For the church is impregnable and irreversible, precisely because it is founded on a

Rock, and that rock is Peter—not in his individual person abstracting from his office, but in his official personality which never dies, being transmitted to each one of his successors. Everything, therefore, diffusively proved about the unity, infallibility, perpetuity, hierarchical organization, and other attributes of the church founded by Jesus Christ, is concentrated and summed up in this one text: "Thou art Peter, and upon this rock I will build my church, and the gates of hell shall not prevail against it."

"And I will give unto thee the keys of the kingdom of heaven." This is another figure or symbol of the delegation of supreme power in the church to Peter. Among the principal nations of antiquity, and particularly among the Hebrews, it was a received usage that the tradition of the keys of the gates of a citadel or city denoted the transfer of dominion over the place itself. Keys made of precious metal and richly ornamented were carried by kings, princes, and magistrates as a symbol of their dignity and authority. In the Hebrew monarchy the grand chancellor of the kingdom, who was the king's vicar and representative, carried a large key on his shoulder as his badge of office. In Isaias (c. xxii.) the Lord says of Eliacim, the son of the high-priest Helcias: "The key of the house of David will I lay upon his shoulder; so he shall open and none shall shut; and he shall shut, and none shall open." This is explained in the context: "Go, get thee unto this treasurer, even unto Shebna, which is over the house, and say, . . . I will drive thee from thy station, . . . and I will call my servant Eliacim, . . . and I will commit thy government into his hand . . . and he shall be for a glorious throne to his father's house." In the Apocalypse the same emblem is used to signify the royalty of Jesus Christ: "These things saith he that is holy, he that is true, he that hath the key of David, he that openeth, and no man shutteth; and shutteth, and no man openeth."* Our Lord, as the lineal descendant of David, was the lawful King of the Jews, which royal lineage was typical of his inherent royalty as Son of God. Therefore the key of David is taken as an emblem of his sovereign dominion over the world. When Christ promised to give his own keys, the keys of his own spiritual kingdom, the symbols of his own sovereign power, to St. Peter, he must have intended to delegate his sovereignty to him, and to constitute him his vicar, with a line of successors to continue as long as his earthly kingdom should last. "And whatsoever thou shalt bind on earth shall be bound in heaven, and whatsoever thou shalt loose on earth shall be loosed in heaven." This is an unlimited

---

* Rev. iii. 7.

and universal power of exercising jurisdiction as a sovereign legislator, judge, and ruler, in the name of God, by divine authority, and with the same obligation over the conscience that inheres in divine laws.

Under a more simple figure, having none of the splendor and magnificence of royalty about it, but yet equally expressive of the power of the sovereign pontificate given to Peter, and more pleasing to the feelings, because it brings out more fully the gentle, beneficent nature of the office of a chief bishop and supreme pastor; Our Lord, after his resurrection, confided the care of his church and his people to his faithful, loving disciple, the predestined bearer of his cross and crown. "Jesus saith to Simon Peter, Simon, son of Jonas, lovest thou me more than these? He saith unto him, Yea, Lord; thou knowest that I love thee. He saith unto him, Feed my lambs. He saith to him again the second time, Simon, son of Jonas, lovest thou me? He saith unto him, Yea, Lord thou knowest that I love thee. He saith unto him, Feed my sheep. He saith unto him the third time, Simon, son of Jonas, lovest thou me? Peter was grieved because he said unto him the third time, Lovest thou me? And he said unto him, Lord, thou knowest all things; thou knowest that I love thee. Jesus saith unto him, Feed my sheep." *

* St. John xxi. 15-17.

This passage, admirably translated as it is in the quaint old English of King James's version, fails in one respect to reproduce the exact force of the original terms. There are two Greek words in it, which are both rendered by the term "feed." One is "boske," which signifies leading to pasture and providing with food. The other is "poimane," which signifies watch, protect, govern. One designates the special office of the shepherd, which is a type of the pastoral office in the church in respect to teaching sound doctrine and morals, giving instruction and exhortation to the faithful, and providing them with sacraments and other wholesome spiritual nutriment. The other designates that part of the pastoral office which belongs to discipline, government, and protection against enemies or other dangers. In Homer and other ancient authors kings are called the shepherds of the people, and *poimane* is used to signify the exercise of the kingly authority. Feeding the flock of Christ includes, therefore, all that belongs to the episcopal office. Feeding the whole flock of Christ denotes the exercise of episcopal supervision over the Catholic Church. There is a distinction made, also, between the sheep and the lambs, indicating that those who have a care over the lesser and weaker members of the flock, and minister to their nourishment—that is, the pastors and bishops, as well as the laity—are committed to the instruction and government of Peter and his successors. He was made pastor over all, bishops, clergy, and people; all of whom, however high their ecclesiastical or civil rank and dignity, kings, primates, and patriarchs, in relation to the Supreme Pastor, are sheep of his flock and his fold. He was made Bishop of bishops, Bishop of the Catholic Church and all its parts and members, which is thus made to constitute One Fold under One Shepherd.

On another occasion, before his passion, Our Lord, in more express and explicit terms, committed the apostles themselves to his care, immediately after he had, in the strongest language he ever used, designated the high and dignified position reserved for them in conjunction with their chief in his kingdom. He gave them first a lesson of humility, proposing himself as an example of that virtue, and cautioning them not to imitate the pride, haughtiness, and domineering spirit usually seen in kings, princes, and other persons of exalted rank. This special recommendation of humility shows that they were to be placed in a position analogous to that of worldly princes, in which they would be exposed to the special temptations which beset the great and powerful. And he says expressly: "I appoint unto you a kingdom, as my Father has appointed unto me." Afterwards, speaking to Peter as the head of the apostolic band, "The Lord said, Simon, Simon, behold, Satan hath desired to have *you* [plural], that he may sift you as wheat: but I have prayed *for thee*, that *thy faith fail not:* and when thou are converted, strengthen thy brethren."* The version of St. Jerome translates this last clause, "et tu, aliquando conversus, confirma fratres tuos," which is literally rendered by the Douay, " thou, being once converted, confirm thy brethren." Some commentators consider the Greek phrase, $\pi o \tau \grave{e} \, \dot{\epsilon} \pi \iota \sigma \tau \rho \acute{\epsilon} \psi \alpha \varsigma$, translated in the common English version, " when thou art converted," as denoting the action of turning towards the apostles like one who is addressing an audience. Let this be as it may, the sense is plain of the whole passage that the special prayer of Christ for an efficacious act of providence and grace to preserve the apostles from the wiles and assaults of Satan was directed upon the person of their chief, Peter. Through the special grace given to him, his unfailing faith was to be the principal means of confirming his brethren. He was specially charged to do this, and the words of Christ are equivalent to a prophecy that he would keep this charge. The sense is analogous to that of the other passage in which the firmness of the rock on which the church is built is set forth as the basis of its impregnable resistance to the gates of hell.

* St. Luke xxii. 25-33.

Literally, Peter and the other apostles are personally the objects of Our Lord's warnings and promises. Everything, however, in the whole passage and its context, has a much deeper and more striking significance, if it is principally referred to the successors of Peter and the apostles. They have had much more of worldly glory, have been much more in danger of being perverted by pride, have had more need to give heed to Our Lord's instructions respecting humility, have been much more violently sifted by Satan, than were the lowly, persecuted, martyred apostles; who were, moreover, confirmed in grace, endowed with inspiration and other miraculous gifts, and made so almost superhuman in virtue that there was scarcely any need of any exercise of authority, or even of any counsel, encouragement, or exhortation, on the part of St. Peter. If we understand the "conversion" of St. Peter to refer to his fall on the occasion of the well-known events preceding the crucifixion of Our Lord, we may understand that Our Lord intended to hint to him beforehand, what he afterwards clearly foretold, that he would make such a manifestation of his own personal weakness as should clearly prove all his subsequent firmness and fidelity to be an effect of the grace of God. The stability of the foundation of the church, the infallibility in faith of the successors of Peter, is thus shown to be supernatural, by the mournful exhibition of his own natural weakness which the very Prince of the Apostles left to all future times as a lesson of humility to the greatest and holiest of the disciples of Christ. We may apply the language of Christ also to those among the successors of St. Peter who have sinned, or have faltered through human weakness in the discharge of their high duties. Repeatedly, in the history of the church, has it been shown that, if the welfare, and even the existence, of the church depended solely on the personal fidelity of the Pope to his sublime trust, both would be in danger. Even the papacy has seemed at times to have been preserved, and the rock of the church to have been kept from being riven asunder, only by a miraculous interposition. In the person of Peter Our Lord addresses all his successors, and in the persons of the apostles all the bishops, until the end of the world. To the Popes he promises that although some of them may be sinners, and others more or less fail to fulfil their duty, their infallibility shall never be compromised by any defection from the faith; and admonishes them, whenever they have yielded, like Peter, to human fear, and failed to face the powers of earth and hell ranged in ferocious array against Christ with due firmness and courage, like Peter to repent and turn back with renewed heroism, to lead on the champions of the faith and law of God to victory. The bishops, and, by consequence, their clergy and people also, are directed toward the indefectible, infallible faith of the successors to Peter's supremacy for confirmation in their own faith, when Satan endeavors to sift them as wheat—that is, when schism, heresy, and apostasy sift out faithless bishops, priests, and people from the mass of the faithful children of the true church.

It is only necessary to have some general knowledge of the history of Christendom to perceive that Our Lord gave in a few words its epitome in his address to the apostles and Peter which we are now considering. This is true in general of all church history, but especially of its most momentous and critical epochs. The unfailing faith of the Successors of Peter, who confirm their brethren in the episcopate in the warfare against heresy and the other hostile powers arrayed against them, and, notwithstanding grievous defections among both the hierarchy and the people, preserve the unity of the church, and triumph successively over all its enemies, is the one grand, salient object which strikes our view. We see the fulfilment of Our Lord's prediction and of his prayer in the fact and the event, and, therefore, we must conclude that he had before his eye as future that which we see as past and present, and that this was the object of his discourse. We may say the same of all that Our Lord, his prophets, and his apostles have declared or foretold concerning the church, its organization, its constitution, its attributes, hierarchy, government, extension, glory, and triumph. It is verified and fulfilled most evidently and completely in the later and more developed periods of the kingdom of Christ on the earth. When an architect exhibits the plan and elevation of a vast, magnificent cathedral, it is a representation of the building in its finished state. We do not look at the building when its foundations are just laid, or its walls half-built, to see the realization of the grand idea in the mind of the architect. We look at the finished structure. If it corresponds to the drawings made beforehand, we ascribe the work to the architect as its author, and we judge that the overseers and artisans employed in building have faithfully executed his design. Just so in the present case. The Holy Scriptures give us plans and pictures of the grand temple of God, the Catholic Church. The scanty historical records of inspired and uninspired writers respecting the first beginnings of Christianity give us only partial glimpses of its inchoate state, when the ground was surveyed and cleared, the materials collected, the foundations laid, the building commenced. A careful inspection will show the fundamental principles of faith, worship, order, and government, the distinctive and ruling idea, the outlines of the plan, as prescribed by the divine Architect and Founder of the church. But we must look to the period of the greatest extension, power, and splendor of the church, in order to behold the actual realization of the divine plan in its completeness. A comparison of the real, actual church with the plan of it laid down in the Holy Scripture, showing an obvious, striking agreement between the two, is the quickest and clearest exhibition of the identity of the Catholic Church of history and of the present time with the church founded by Jesus Christ and builded by the apostles and their successors in the primitive ages.

I have already shown from the prophets, and from the apostles and evangelists, partly speaking as they were personally taught by the Son of God, and reciting his own words, and partly giving utterance to what he taught them by his Holy Spirit, what the principles, attributes, and outward notes of the true church of God, as the kingdom of Christ on earth, really are, as revealed in the Holy Scriptures. This has been done with the intention of pointing out to the sincere believer in the Holy Scriptures the true Way of Salvation in the true church. I have nothing more to do now than to point to the grand, historical, Catholic Church of Nice, Chalcedon, Florence, Trent, and the Vatican; the church now and always united as a well-organized body politic and kingdom under the supremacy of the Successor of Peter, and to say: See there! the kingdom of God foretold by Isaias, founded by Jesus Christ on the Rock of Peter, against which the gates of hell have never prevailed, and shall never prevail. In the great church of the Fathers and Councils, the church of the fourth and fifth centuries; in the church of the thirteenth century and the whole mediæval period; and in no other, can we find any adequate fulfilment of the superb and glowing descriptions of the kingdom of God given by Isaias and the other prophets. I have known plain people, brought up Presbyterians in the remote parts of New England, to be struck with this obvious parallel, merely by reading attentively the prophets and some popular histories written in English. The great Christendom, with its wonderful civilization and political order, proceeding from, and governed by the spiritual order, under the universal and beneficent monarchy of the Pope, which arose on the ruins of the great precedent empires, and is just now going to pieces, is the only fact which presents even an appearance of a reign of Christ and the saints on the earth. What can the Rock of Peter be, except the Roman Church? The whole history of that church, and of the entire catholic communion under its supremacy, is an illustration and fulfilment of the words of Christ: "On this Rock I will build my church, and the gates of hell shall not prevail against it." Its history since the great churches of the East finally went down and the great apostasy in the West took place, and its present attitude since the Council of the Vatican was assembled, are only more palpable and wonderful illustrations of the same divine prophecy. Let the devout adorer of Jesus Christ, who believes that his word is the word of God, attentively consider that word which he spoke to Peter, and look upon the church which is at this day governed by the Successor of Peter, and ask his conscience if he can refuse to acknowledge the holy, catholic, apostolic, Roman Church as the one, true church founded by Jesus Christ, and its supreme head as his Vicar.

The obligation of obedience to the Catholic Church, and the necessity of being in her communion and receiving the sacraments from her lawful ministers, in order to be justified and saved, follow from the simple fact that she is the true and only church established by Jesus Christ. This ought to be so plain to any one who has followed the steps of my argument as to require no further proof, nor even one word of remark. Nevertheless, those who are brought up under the influence of Lutheran and Calvinistic doctrines find it very hard to see into the vital importance of the question of the true church, or to understand the obligation and necessity of being a member of that church when it is once ascertained. The reason is that they have always believed that justification and salvation are purely individual matters between the soul of each one and God, which are settled without the mediation of any church, or priest, or any kind of human intervention. The visible church becomes therefore, for them, only a useful institution for keeping up common worship, providing for public instruction, carrying on benevolent works, and in general promoting religious and moral improvement. Quite naturally, having this notion of the church, they say that they cannot see how the particular form of church government, the mode of ordination, or the ceremonies of worship can be of essential and vital importance to salvation. They may admit the importance of harmony, co-operation, and union in a general sense among Christians. But they do not admit that it is necessary for all who are true Christians to be members of one true church which is exclusive in its organization. They speak about different ways leading to the same term, varieties of form which do not belong to the essence of religion, and in many other ways show that they look on the church and all else that is visible and incorporate in Christianity as something merely exterior and indifferent, having no vital and essential relation to the interior and spiritual part For this class of persons the arguments which are sufficient to a high-churchman are wholly deficient and inefficacious. These arguments usually presuppose an idea which is wanting in the doctrine of the Calvinistic sects. They are constructed with a view to prove from Scripture and history the external constitution of the church. The question is about the orders of the hierarchy, the authority of bishops, councils, the Roman primacy, etc., just as in civil matters the origin and nature of imperial, royal, aristocratic, and republican governments are discussed. The external side of the church, as the kingdom of Christ on earth, its power and glory, its humanizing and civilizing influences, its splendor of science and art, the wisdom of its jurisprudence, and other things similar to these, are made prominent. These are all very important and interesting matters. Yet there are many Protestants in these later times who can more or less appreciate and admire them, make a very just estimate of the Catholic Church in the past ages, and even look forward to some new epoch in which all Christians will in some way come together and carry on the work of the past through the future, without ever thinking of really embracing the Catholic faith and communion. Such a man was Leibnitz, and such were

Guizot and Leo, besides a multitude of others, who stand around the walls of the city of God, admire them, and yet think they are quite safe in their own little villages where they were born and brought up.

The serious and pious reader of these pages will therefore please to reflect that I have throughout only so far touched on the outward part of the church as the exigency of my great topic required, which was the way of interior justification and eternal salvation in and through the soul of the church, its spiritual and principal part, of which the visible hierarchy and sacraments are the organs and instruments. Let him reflect on the whole course of thought and argument which I have pursued, and he will see that I have refuted the primary falsehood of Luther and Calvin, that each man is justified immediately and at once by a private and personal relation which is established between himself and Christ. I have proved that the relation between Christ and men, as Redeemer and redeemed, is generic, not individual; and is initial only, not complete, until certain conditions have been verified. I have also proved that this relation, generic in its inchoate, initial state, is generic in its actual and complete form—that is, that it produces an organic society, superseding the one first instituted, into which the individual members are introduced by regeneration. I have proved that faith is the first personal condition and prerequisite for regeneration, and that this faith presupposes an official, authoritative, and infallible teaching of divine truths by the hierarchy of the church; also, that obedience to the law of God, as promulgated, explained, and applied by the same authority, is another obligatory condition of obtaining, preserving, and increasing justification; that one part of this law requires that the regenerate man, having received regeneration through the sacrament of baptism, should obtain remission of sin and other graces through sacraments lawfully administered in the church. The conditions of justification, therefore, absolutely require that one should obey the authority of the Catholic Church lodged in the hands of the Vicar of Christ, and the bishops whose jurisdiction is derived from his supreme power. The very first condition is faith, and faith demands a submission of the mind and will to all that the church commands, in the name of God, the faithful to believe. The church teaches and commands through her hierarchy. The head of the hierarchy is the Pope, the supreme teacher and lawgiver who succeeds to the supremacy given by Christ to Peter. The catechumen must therefore learn from him, through his own particular instructor, what are the things necessary to salvation.

When Christ gave to Peter and his successors supreme power to teach and command, he imposed on all who know that this power was given a corresponding obligation to believe and obey. The Vicar of Jesus Christ teaches the catechumen at the very outset that he must receive baptism from no other person but a priest authorized by him, under the penalty of grievous sin and sacrilege. By the very fact of baptism he becomes the subject of the lawful pastors who are authorized by the Supreme Pastor, and much more of the Supreme Pastor himself. This subjection is perpetual, and revolt from it separates the rebel from the church. Once baptized, he must keep the precepts of the church, and receive the sacraments from her lawful and authorized ministers. If he communicates with heretics and schismatics, he incurs at once the guilt of mortal sin, the penalty of excommunication, and thereby exclusion from the kingdom of heaven, whose keys are in the hand of the Successor of St. Peter. It does not alter the case at all if the pastors whom he follows have received personally, or through their predecessors, priestly or episcopal ordination from Catholic bishops. Their assemblies, their worship, their administration of sacraments, are unlawful and sacrilegious. The Vicar of Christ is the supreme judge, whose judgments are ratified in heaven. It is for him to decide which are the lawful bishops, and which particular churches are parts of the true Catholic Church. He condemns all heretics and schismatics, all who are not of the holy, catholic, apostolic, Roman Church, whether they have valid orders or not. It is, therefore, obligatory and necessary for the catechumen who knows which the true church is, not only to receive baptism, but to receive it from a Catholic priest; to receive, likewise, instruction, remission of sins in the sacrament of penance, holy communion, and the other sacraments, not only from one who is really a priest or bishop, but from one who has lawful jurisdiction in the Catholic Church.

If a person has received baptism, either with or without any fault of his own, from a minister who is not authorized by the church, and if he is a member of a sect, whether it be a schismatical body like the so-called Greek Church, or any of the heretical sects of Protestantism, he is, nevertheless, by his baptism a lawful subject of the Catholic Church. If he be innocent of any wilful fault in the matter, he is a lamb of the flock committed by Christ to Peter, astray from the true fold. When he finds out his error, he is bound to return immediately to his true and lawful pastor. If he has strayed away by his own fault, or if he persists in staying out after he has discovered his error, he is a rebel, and is bound to repent and return to obedience, as the only condition of salvation. All the baptized are already the subjects of the Vicar of Christ, and all the unbaptized are bound to receive baptism and become his subjects. This follows necessarily from what I have proved; that Christ has established his church under the form of a visible kingdom subject to the supremacy of St. Peter and his successors, as the Way of Salvation, the King's Highway leading to heaven; and has commanded all mankind to enter into it, and to walk in it to everlasting life.

There are some persons who put aside all the evidence of the divine authority of the Catholic Church, and close their ears to all persuasion to obey the commandment of Christ by entering into his true fold, in some such way as the following. They say: "My mother was a good, holy woman; therefore the religion in which she lived and died is good enough for me." This might be a sensible reason for one who could not find anything better or more certain to go by. But it is utterly senseless and absurd when it is used as an argument wherewith to break the force of evidence and shut out the light of divine truth. Do such persons believe that there is any revealed doctrine and any law which all men are bound to believe and obey, when they know them? Do they think that they alone have had good mothers? Such reasoning would prevent every person whose parents were virtuous, or who saw that there were virtuous and good people in the religion he had been bred up in, from admitting any evidence, however conclusive, that the religion of his fathers is defective or erroneous. It seems ridiculous to take serious notice of such a frivolous and absurd notion. Yet I have heard it gravely proposed, not only by simple and uneducated people, but by the most intelligent persons. Therefore it is that I take the trouble to answer it seriously. Surely, my dear friend, you must see that it is foolish and impious for you to make any reply or objection whatever to a commandment of your Sovereign Lord, Jesus Christ. Who are you, and who are your parents, or all those men who seem to you most worthy of respect and honor, in comparison with Him? Will you set their opinions against his declaration, or their seeming goodness against his sanctity, and follow their footsteps as more secure marks of the true way than the directions which he has given you? The truth of the divine revelation is absolutely certain; and to one who has divine faith it is above any natural truth whatever, excluding all fear or possibility of error, and resting on the veracity of God himself. The opinion which one may have of the holiness and the eternal salvation of particular persons is not by any means so certain. Let us suppose, however, that those parents or other persons whose memory you revere so much were really holy and are now in heaven. If they were holy, they would have submitted to the authority of the true church, in case it had been sufficiently proposed to them, if they had been true to the ruling principle of their lives; that is, to obey God when his will was made known to them. If they are in heaven, they know that the Catholic Church is the true church, they are members of it in the triumphant state of glory; and if they were allowed to speak to you, they would tell you to become members of the same church militant on earth. Because certain persons have been all their lives outside of the visible communion of the true church without any fault of their own, it does not follow that you can remain outside without fault. Some persons are ignorant of the divinity of Jesus Christ, or even of his existence. They are, therefore, not to blame for their want of explicit faith in him. But if you do not believe in him and in his words, you are guilty of sin, and will be condemned to eternal punishment, unless you repent and believe. Supposing that some persons who have never had explicit faith in the Catholic Church, or made explicit profession of obedience to her authority, may have been saved by an implicit faith and by obedience to that part of the divine law which was known to them, yet this does not help those who refuse to believe and obey the church by their own wilfulness. Whoever is saved is saved by faith and the love of God, and is united to the soul of the church by sanctifying grace. But no one can have faith who refuses to believe any one doctrine of the faith which is sufficiently proposed to him. No one can have the love of God who disobeys one of his commandments which has been made known to him. No one can receive sanctifying grace through any other channel than the sacrament of baptism lawfully administered in the church; or preserve it unless he receives the other sacraments, keeps the precepts of the church, and remains in her communion as a docile and obedient child; if he knows which is the true church, and who is the true pastor commissioned by Jesus Christ, and has the opportunity and the ability to approach those sacraments which Christ has instituted as the only ordinary means of grace and salvation. Supposing, therefore, that you have dear friends in heaven, who have been saved by extraordinary grace; your only hope of rejoining them hereafter is bound to the condition that you use faithfully the ordinary and appointed means which God has placed in the one, true church. Perhaps the mother of St. Paul was saved and met him in heaven, though it is most likely that she never explicitly believed in Jesus as the true Messias or received the sacrament of baptism. Yet St. Paul would have been damned if he had not believed and been baptized.

The same objection, in another form, is only repeated when persons fall back on their own experience. They have found what their souls need, they say, in the religion they have been brought up in. They believe in Jesus Christ, find comfort in the Bible and in prayer, profit in sermons and spiritual books, have a conscience at rest and a hope of being saved. What more do they need or can they wish for? Why is it so necessary to be received into another church, even if it be a grand and admirable church, quite sufficient for those who are bred up in it or who prefer to join it? The answer is nearly the same as the one just given. Granted, that you have heretofore believed with sincerity what you have been taught, that you have lived up to your light, that you have received many graces; what then? Is the evidence I have given of the exclusive right of the Catholic Church to your obedience conclusive? If it is—and it is, most assuredly—you have received now a new light, and incurred a new obligation. If Our Lord should personally appear to you, and command you to believe all the church teaches and fulfil all she commands, as the indispensable condition of salvation, would you dare to hesitate and make objections on the ground I have mentioned? Jesus Christ speaks to you from heaven through his word, through his church, through the bishops and the Supreme Pastor of the church, the successors of the apostles and St. Peter. " See that you refuse not him that speaketh. For if they escaped not who refused him that spake on earth, *much more shall not we escape, if we turn away from him that speaketh from heaven.*" * " He who saith that he knoweth him, and keepeth not his commandments, is a liar, and the truth is not in him." † If the truth has been in you heretofore, and even if you have lived without any grievous sin until now, the truth will depart from you, you will become false, and you will incur the guilt of mortal sin, whose penalty is eternal condemnation, unless you obey the truth now presented to you, and proved by the Scripture which you profess to revere. Do you not know that Our Lord has commanded you to hear and obey those whom he has sent, as himself; that he has said that those who hear them hear him, and those who despise them despise him and the Father who sent him? I have proved to you that the Catholic bishops are sent by Christ; that the Successor of St. Peter is the Vicar of Christ upon earth; that the keys of the kingdom of heaven and supreme power of teaching and ruling are in his hands. Therefore, if you refuse to believe his teaching and obey his authority, and to come into his fold under

* Hebrews xii. 25.   † 1 Epistle St. John ii. 4.

the pastors whom he has appointed, you reject, despise, and disobey Christ and God.

As for those who say right out that all religions are alike, that all persons cannot have the same religion, that it is no matter what a person believes, I cannot, stop, at present, to reason with them. It is incredible that sensible persons can utter such nonsense. Plainly, they can make no pretence of being Christians at all. It is therefore useless to prove to them what true Christianity is, and what Christ teaches and commands. They are sceptics, like Pontius Pilate, and repeat his sceptical question, "What is truth?" Such persons need a different treatment from that which is suitable for the class of readers I have at present in view. For these, it is sufficient to show what the Holy Scriptures teach, or what may be proved by them, if they are consistent and upright in their profession of belief in them. It is this perfect sincerity and uprightness which is chiefly requisite, in order that one who has the evidence of the Catholic religion proposed to him may be convinced by it, and act on his conviction. Fidelity to the light of reason, to the glimmerings of divine illumination, to the voice of conscience; earnestness in obeying the will of God and seeking for the salvation of the soul; are the great requisites for obtaining the full and clear light of faith and the efficacious grace which brings the enquirer into the royal road of salvation. Unhappily, they are too often wanting. Reason is silenced, the inspirations of grace are resisted, conscience is stifled, because prejudice, old habits and associations, worldly interests, human affections, moral cowardice, the fear of making sacrifices, are arrayed against them, and bind the captive soul in a willing bondage under the accustomed dominion of its old errors. Therefore many who are not far from the kingdom of God never enter into it. Converts to the Catholic Church have been numerous in these latter days, but the number of those who have felt the first motions of the grace of conversion, and have drawn back, is much greater. It is easy to see that their great obstacle has not been a want of sufficient light to see the truth, or a lack of evidence to convince the intellect, but a want of sincerity and moral courage to rise up, leave all worldly interests behind them, and follow Christ in the way of the cross. The strength and durability of Protestantism, at the present time, do not so much consist in the positive conviction of its adherents that their particular sects possess the pure and perfect doctrines and institutions of the primitive and apostolic Christianity, as in the political and social interests and temporal goods with which it is interwoven. It has made to itself a domain and kingdom after the semblance of the Catholic Church. It has its antiquity, its traditions, its heroes, historical associations, universities, literature, sacred burial-places, great benevolent institutions, vast wealth, and a multitude of places where studious and quiet men find a pleasant employment and a respectable living. Wherever it is dominant, those who embrace the Catholic faith are obliged to sever their connection more or less with their native world, and migrate to another and a strange sphere. For many, and especially for the married Protestant clergy, the profession of the Catholic faith involves great sacrifices. Besides those which are necessary from the very nature of the case, there are many others to which persons who desire to become Catholics are subjected by the persecution of their former associates in religion, and of those with whom they are socially connected. Converts have been ostracized from their families and society, calumniated, disinherited, driven from their employments, treated as disgraced and criminal persons, forcibly prevented from practising their religion, driven into poverty, and otherwise made the victims of social and domestic tyranny; in spite of the pretence which Protestants make of respecting liberty of conscience. And numbers of others who were convinced that they ought to become Catholics, and who wished to do so, have been prevented by unjust and violent means, by threats, or by a well-grounded fear of suffering ill-treatment, from obeying the voice of their conscience. Those who are separated from the Catholic Church are suffering for the sins of their forefathers. They abandoned the glorious and peaceful kingdom of Christ, and wandered away to found new churches after the devices of their own hearts. The return is therefore difficult and painful for their descendants, like the return of the children of Israel to Chanaan after their captivity.

I beg leave to represent to all the intelligent and serious Protestants who read these pages that, hard as it is for them to give up all those things connected with their religion which are so dear to them, it is better that they should do so voluntarily, while they have time to save what is left to them of their ancient Catholic heritage. The churches of Protestantism are built on the sand, and their unstable foundations are rapidly being undermined and washed away by the encroaching tide of infidelity and impiety. The Bible is fast losing the authority which belongs to it, but which cannot stand long without the support of the church. The remnants of the Catholic creed are fast dissolving, and the ancient Christian laws of morality loosening their hold. Protestant orthodoxy is crumbling to pieces before our eyes, and the descendants of those who were the most zealous workmen in building and extending it are the most active agents in the work of tearing down the structure of their fathers. The men of the present generation may console themselves with the hope that it will outlast their time. It is to be feared that the majority of them will do so, and will remain where they are; unless some special intervention of God shall speedily open their eyes to see that the Catholic Church is the only refuge of salvation for society in general, and for every individual who wishes to escape the destroying flood of impiety. For the coming generation the alternative of the Catholic faith or no religion is certain, imperative, and inevitable. Those for whom I am chiefly writing profess to obey the will of God before all other things, to believe in Jesus Christ as the Divine Saviour of men, and to follow his teachings and precepts. Let them reflect on his words and on the examples of the apostles and primitive Christians. "Seek ye, therefore, first the kingdom of God, and his righteousness." "He that loveth father or mother more than me is not worthy of me: and he that loveth son or daughter more than me is not worthy of me. And he that taketh not up his cross, and followeth after me, is not worthy of me. He that findeth his life shall lose it: and he that shall lose his life for my sake shall find it."* The enquiry after the true church, the true faith, the lawful sacraments, is not one of secondary importance, relating to non-essential matters. It is a question of life and death, an enquiry after the true and

---

* St. Matthew vi. 33; x. 37, 39.

only way of salvation established by Jesus Christ. The only consideration admissible by any upright and conscientious person who fears God and wishes to save his soul is: What is the truth, what is my duty? The only honest decision, when these are ascertained, is to follow them immediately, without regard to any temporal motives or interests. Such was the conduct of our first Christian ancestors; and it has been imitated by many in our own day, whose noble and generous loyalty to conscience and the faith once delivered to the saints is a grand offset to the ignoble apostasies of faithless and fallen Christians who have deserted the glorious standard of the cross. May the grace of God add daily to their number, and bring back all the strayed lambs of Christ who still reverence his name and word to the fold of the true church, that there may be one fold and one shepherd, and the prayer of Christ receive its perfect fulfilment: "That they all may be one; as thou, Father, art in me, and I in thee, that they also may be one in us."